First World War

and Army of Occupation

War Diary

France, Belgium and Germany

7 INDIAN (MEERUT) DIVISION
Divisional Troops
4 Brigade Royal Field Artillery
31 August 1914 - 11 December 1915

WO95/3936/2

The Naval & Military Press Ltd
www.nmarchive.com
Published in association with The National Archives

Published by

The Naval & Military Press Ltd

Unit 10 Ridgewood Industrial Park,
Uckfield, East Sussex,
TN22 5QE England
Tel: +44 (0) 1825 749494

www.naval-military-press.com
www.nmarchive.com

This diary has been reprinted in facsimile from the original. Any imperfections are inevitably reproduced and the quality may fall short of modern type and cartographic standards.

Contents

Document type	Place/Title	Date From	Date To
Heading	WO95/3936/2 4 Brigade Royal Field Artillery		
Heading	7 Meerut Division Jan-Oct 1915 4 Bde R.F.A. 1914 Aug-1915 Oct		
Heading	IV Bde R.F.A. Head Quarters VII Btty Sep-Nov XIV Btty Ammn Column		
Miscellaneous	War Diary		
War Diary	Trimulgherry	31/08/1914	26/10/1914
Heading	War Diary of 4th Bde R.F.A. Headquarters From 27.10.14 To 30/11/14 Volume PP		
War Diary	Orleans Camp Les Grouse	27/10/1914	30/11/1914
Heading	War Diary of Headquarters 4th Bde RFA From 1-12-14 To 31-12-14 Volume		
War Diary		01/12/1914	31/12/1914
Heading	War Diary of 7th Battery R.F.A. From 1-9-14 To 30-11-14 Pp 1 To 7 Volume I		
War Diary	Trimulgherry Deccan	01/09/1914	01/11/1914
War Diary	Near Richebourg St Vaast	02/11/1914	30/11/1914
Map	Map		
Heading	Indian Army Corps 66th Batty R.F.A. Vol I 31.8.14-20.10.14		
War Diary		31/08/1914	20/10/1914
Heading	14th Battery RFA War Diary From 31-8-1914 to 7-1-1915		
War Diary	Secunderabad	31/08/1914	15/09/1914
War Diary	Bombay	16/09/1914	20/09/1914
War Diary	At Sea	20/09/1914	20/09/1914
War Diary	Port Sury	03/10/1914	07/10/1914
War Diary	Marseilles	14/10/1914	18/10/1914
War Diary	Orleans	20/10/1914	27/10/1914
War Diary	Merville	29/10/1914	29/10/1914
War Diary	Les Facons	30/10/1914	30/10/1914
War Diary	Rue Les Chavattes	31/10/1914	03/11/1914
War Diary	Le Touret	04/11/1914	06/11/1914
War Diary	Les Chavattes	07/11/1914	03/12/1914
War Diary	Le Touret	04/12/1914	13/12/1914
War Diary	St Vaast	14/12/1914	17/12/1914
War Diary	Le Touret	17/12/1914	17/12/1914
War Diary	Paradis	18/12/1914	25/12/1914
War Diary	Ames	26/12/1914	07/01/1915
Heading	War Diary of 4th Brigade Ammunition Column R.F.A. From 31-8-14 To 30-11-14 Volume I		
War Diary		24/10/1914	29/11/1914
Heading	War Diary of 4th Brigade R.F.A. Gun Col From 1-12-14 To 31-12-14 Volume I		
War Diary	Le Casan	01/12/1914	12/12/1914
War Diary	La Couture	13/12/1914	16/12/1914
War Diary	Robecq	17/12/1914	25/12/1914
War Diary	Ames	26/12/1914	31/12/1914
War Diary	Trimulgherry	31/08/1914	19/09/1914
War Diary	Un Ships	20/09/1914	14/10/1914

War Diary	Marseilles	15/10/1914	19/10/1914
War Diary	Orleans	20/10/1914	30/10/1914
War Diary	Merville	31/10/1914	31/10/1914
War Diary	Les Facons	01/11/1914	08/11/1914
War Diary	Le Casan	09/11/1914	30/11/1914
Heading	War Diary of 56th Battery R.F.A. From 1st January 1915 To 31st January 1915		
War Diary	Lespesses	01/01/1915	25/01/1915
War Diary	Calonne	26/01/1915	26/01/1915
War Diary	Croix-Barbee	27/01/1915	31/01/1915
Heading	War Diary of 4th Brigade R.F.A. From 1-1-15 To 31-1-15		
War Diary		01/01/1915	31/01/1915
Heading	Feb 1915 4th Bde R.F.A.		
Miscellaneous	On His Majesty's Service.		
Miscellaneous	IV Brigade R.F.A.		
Heading	War Diary of 4th Brigade R.F.A. From 1st February 1915 To 28th February 1915		
War Diary		01/02/1915	28/02/1915
Heading	War Diary of IV Brigade R.F.A. From 1st March 1915 To 31st March 1915		
War Diary		01/03/1915	31/03/1915
Heading	War Diary of IV Brigade R.F.A. From 1st April 1915 To 30th April 1915		
War Diary		01/04/1915	30/04/1915
Heading	War Diary of IV Brigade R.F.A. From 1st May 1915 To 31st May 1915		
War Diary		01/05/1915	31/05/1915
Heading	War Diary of IV Brigade R.F.A. From 1st June 1915 To 30th June 1915		
War Diary		01/06/1915	30/06/1915
Heading	War Diary of IV Brigade R.F.A. From 1st July 1915 To 31st July 1915		
War Diary		01/07/1915	31/07/1915
Heading	War Diary of IV Brigade R.F.A. From 1st August 1915 To 31st August 1915		
War Diary		01/08/1915	31/08/1915
Heading	War Diary of IV Brigade R.F.A. From 1st September 1915 To 30th September 1915		
War Diary		01/09/1915	30/09/1915
Heading	War Diary of IV Brigade R.F.A. From 1st October 1915 To 31st October 1915		
War Diary		01/10/1915	31/10/1915
War Diary	War Diary of the Officer Commanding IV Brigade R.F.A. From November 1st 1915 To November 30th 1915 (Volume--)		
War Diary		01/11/1915	30/11/1915
Heading	War Diary For December 1915 4th Brigade R.F.A.		
War Diary	Nedonchelle	01/12/1915	11/12/1915

[illegible]

[illegible]

7 Meerut Division
JAN - OCT. 1915

4 BDE R.F.A.

1914 AUG — 1915 OCT

T. 3 (LAHORE) DIV
MESOPOTAMIA

IV BDE R.F.A

HEAD QUARTERS

VII BTTY SEP-NOV.

XIV BTTY

AMMN COLUMN.

Section. 3 File No. 272

Heading. War Diaries Serial No.

NOTES. 121/1641

Pros. 19 Nos.

SUBJECT.

War diary of Hd Qrs 4th Brigade R.F.A.

LAHORE DIVISION

From.

IV Bde R.F.A.

No. Aug — Oct 1914 Recd.

General. Diary. Register. No. Enclos. Spare Copies.

Brief Abstract of letter.

Notes and Orders.

Period 31/8/ to 26.10.14

Army Form C. 2118.

Instructions regarding War Diaries and Intelligence Summaries are contained in F. S. Regs., Part II, and the Staff Manual respectively. Title pages will be prepared in manuscript.

WAR DIARY

or

INTELLIGENCE SUMMARY.

(Erase heading not required.)

Hour, Date, Place.	Summary of Events and Information.	Remarks and references to Appendices.

Gulab Singh & Sons, Calcutta—No. 22 Army C.—5-8-14—1,07,000.

Army Form C. 2118.

Instructions regarding War Diaries and Intelligence Summaries are contained in F. S. Regs., Part II, and the Staff Manual respectively. Title pages will be prepared in manuscript.

WAR DIARY
or
INTELLIGENCE SUMMARY.
(*Erase heading not required.*)

Hour, Date, Place.	Summary of Events and Information.	Remarks and references to Appendices.
30 Sept 1914	One more horse 7th Battery R.F.A. died of heat on Subadar.	RBB
2 . 10 . 1914	Passed the "Brothers" in Gulf of Suez.	
6 am 3 . 10 . 1914	Arrived at Suez an anchored near head of convoy. Taroba received 160 sacks bran from Cairo. Remained all day at Suez.	RBB. RBB
4 am 4 . 10 . 14.	Entered Suez Canal which was guarded by H.L.I. & Gurkhas.	
5 30 pm –	Arrived Port Said & took up berth near Oil tanks about 1½ mile from Customs House. Subadar & Knight Companion still at Suez	RBB.
5 . 10 . 1914	Officers & W.O. allowed on Shore. Further supply of potatoes onions & bran received. Five native drivers XIII Bde sent to S.S. Haveldar.	RBB
6 . 10 . 1914	Subadar & Knight Companion arrived. Two Corporals transferred to former & 3 Indian Ranks Indore Transport Corps & one Indian Driver 9th A.C. R.F.A. to latter. Twelve transports escorted by the French battleship "Jaurie Guiberry" left Port Said. 2nd Lieut Anderson & one man 7th Battery put ashore at Suez with dysentery on 4th & 6th instant. Two horses on Knight Companion died (1 hor 14th Bty) (1 h 9th AC)	RBB
7 . 10 . 14.	Taroba. Subadar & Knight Companion formed second convoy collecting off Port Said. Convoy sailed at 2 30 pm in fine weather escorted by French battleship "Bouvet"	RBB.

Army Form C. 2118.

WAR DIARY

or

INTELLIGENCE SUMMARY.

(*Erase heading not required.*)

Instructions regarding War Diaries and Intelligence Summaries are contained in F. S. Regs., Part II, and the Staff Manual respectively. Title pages will be prepared in manuscript.

Hour, Date, Place.	Summary of Events and Information.	Remarks and references to Appendices.
8th October 1914	One horse 7th Battery was destroyed on 5th suffering from paralysis. Convoy still in fine weather by Great [illegible]	[illegible]
10 – 10 – 1914	One horse 7th Battery died	
11 – 10 – 1914	Troopships Dilwara, Dongola & Somali left convoy for Malta	[illegible]
14 – 10 – 1914	Arrived Marseilles 3·45 pm. & received instructions to disembark	[illegible]

[illegible signature]
Lieut Colonel RFA
Comdg IV Bde RFA

Gulab Singh & Sons, Calcutta—No. 22 Army C.—5-8-14—1,07,000.

Army Form C. 2118.

Instructions regarding War Diaries and Intelligence Summaries are contained in F. S. Regs., Part II, and the Staff Manual respectively. Title pages will be prepared in manuscript.

WAR DIARY

or

INTELLIGENCE SUMMARY.

(Erase heading not required.)

Hour, Date, Place.	Summary of Events and Information.	Remarks and references to Appendices.
14 - 10 - 14	Disembarked mule of Sudore Transport Corps during evening also some stores. The arrival of units 4th Bde reported at Base Office on S.S. Charles Roux.	RBW
15 - 10 - 14	Disembarkation completed & 4th Bde marched out to Camp at Parc Borelly (on race course) 4 miles from the Quay. Very heavy rain storm during the night flooded the whole camp.	RBW
16 - 10 - 14	Bde remained in Camp. New rifle drawn & ammunition changed also warm service clothing. Heavy rain came on again in evening & completely flooded the camp.	RBW
17 - 10 - 14	Received orders to Entrain. Left spare kit at Base Depôt	RBW
5 p.m.	Left camp & marched to landing sheds near S.S. Charles Roux	
9.30 pm	Marched to La Gare L'Arenc with 7th Batty RFA & began entraining at 10.30 pm in the train	
18 - 10 - 14 6.5 am	Left Marseilles for Orleans via Mountpellier	RBW
20 - 10 - 14 10.30 am	Arrived Orleans detrained & marched to Camp Les Groues	RBW
26 10 14	Received orders for Head Qrs 4th Bde, 7th & 14th batteries to proceed on 27th & 66th Bty & 4 Bde Am Column early on 28th.	RBW

Gulab Singh & Sons, Calcutta—No. 22 Army C.—5-8-14—1,07,000.

War Diary

of

4th Bn R [illegible]

From 27 [illegible]

to 30 [illegible]

[illegible]

Instructions regarding War Diaries and Intelligence Summaries are contained in F. S. Regs., Part II, and the Staff Manual respectively. Title pages will be prepared in manuscript.

Army Form C. 2118.

WAR DIARY
or
INTELLIGENCE SUMMARY.
(Erase heading not required.)

4th Bde R.F.A.

Hour, Date, Place.	Summary of Events and Information.	Remarks and references to Appendices.
27 - 10 = 14 Orleans Camp les Groues	Capt Turnbull joined 14th Bty on 20th Oct. Lieut Pritchard joined 25th. ~~Comm leave~~ Capt Potter joined 7th Bty from 28th also Lieut Gage. Lieut Chance joined 66th Bty from ~~another~~ 19th battery on 25th Oct	RAW
5-40	Headqrs 4th Bde + 7th Batty Entrained on same train at Les Merlins Station Orleans	
28 - 10 - 14	Passed Calais in the train	RAW
29th - 10 - 14. 10am 11-pm	Reached LILLERS + detrained. Vide French map of ST OMER No 4. 1" = 1·26 miles Marched to MERVILLE via ST VENANT. The men billeted in a Saw mill officers in houses in the village	RAW
30th - 10 - 14 7.30am	Head Qrs Bde, O.C.s Batteries rode out to 20th Infy Bde Head Quarters at Cse du Roux E of BETHUNE, to take over from 27 Bde R.F.A already in action there. The batteries moved to LES GLATIGNES & bivouacked. The Colonel & Adjutant remained at Cse du Roux vide MAP OF ARRAS. No 7	RAW
31 - 10 - 14	The 7th Bty were in reserve at village west of RUE DES CHAVATTES	
7-am	"14th Bty took up position previously occupied by 121st Battery at 7am. They engaged enemys advancing infantry at 1-35 pm fired 38 rounds. The 66th Bty took up position from 119th Bty, only 15 rounds fired. The 37th Bty remaining from 5th Div Artillery fired 36 Shrapnel.	RAW
11.15	Heavy firing from direction LA QUINQUE RUE. 14th, 66th + 37th opened fire in support + the firing subsided. During the night 3 attacks took place and some ground was lost & partly retaken	
1 - 11 - 14	The batteries fire was very effective + gave great relief to infantry who had a fairly quiet day followed by a quiet night. Some German heavy guns were located + silenced by 37 Howitzer battery whilst 66 + 14 batteries shelled trenches in German position with great effect.	RAW

G.

Gulab Singh & Sons, Calcutta—No. 22 Army C.—5-8-14—1,07,000.

Army Form C. 2118.

Instructions regarding War Diaries and Intelligence Summaries are contained in F. S. Regs., Part II, and the Staff Manual respectively. Title pages will be prepared in manuscript.

WAR DIARY
or
INTELLIGENCE SUMMARY.
(*Erase heading not required.*)

Hour, Date, Place.	Summary of Events and Information.	Remarks and references to Appendices.
2-11-14	No serious attack took place. 7th Bty observing party [illegible] twice shelled out. Heavy shell from Germans fell near H.Q. in afternoon. Situation generally quiet.	
3-11-14	16th Battery fired 75 shell in preparation for an attack which did not come off. Otherwise situation quiet. A few shell fell near 37th How Battery horse lines in afternoon. The 66th observation station was twice shelled out. At 10 pm the 7th Bty assisted in repulse of an attack on the Connaught Rifles on our left wing. The fire of the batteries has been effective.	
4-11-14 12.22	7th & 66th Batteries fired on a battery enfilading 2/3 Connaught Rifles assisted by 37 Howitzer battery.	
2.30	7th Bty fired on German trenches in front of Seaforths who were being attacked heavily. 66th Battery supported 1/34 & 2/39 who were attacked. 16th Battery in reserve. Secondary positions were reconnoitred & are in course of preparation near LE TOURET. The 11th Bde A.C. remained at LES LOBES about 2 miles W. of [illegible]. 7th Bty fired on Germans collecting in front of 2/39 G.R.	
5-11-14 11.30am	7th Bty shelled enemy digging trenches & afterwards cooperated in action on right of our Brigade & left of 21st Infantry Bde which was reported to have been pushed back. They fired 103 rounds. 66th Battery silenced enemy's guns twice & shelled German trenches near LA QUEQUE RUE.	
4pm	Enemy shelled battery close behind [illegible] Quarters very heavily during afternoon & preparations to leave H.Q. had to be made but were cancelled on the shell fire stopping at 4-20 pm.	

Gulab Singh & Sons, Calcutta—No. 22 Army C.—5-8-14—1,07,000.

Instructions regarding War Diaries and Intelligence Summaries are contained in F. S. Regs., Part II, and the Staff Manual respectively. Title pages will be prepared in manuscript.

WAR DIARY

or

INTELLIGENCE SUMMARY.

(Erase heading not required.)

Army Form C. 2118.

Hour, Date, Place.		Summary of Events and Information.	Remarks and references to Appendices.
6-11-14	3.am	Enemy attacked left & left centre of 20th Infantry Bde. & 7th Battery opened fire. The attack was repulsed. 6am Fresh attack of left	
	6 am	66th & 7th fired on enemys trenches & stopped their advance	
	5.40 pm	5.40. 7th & 66th Batteries fired, 7th on trenches in centre in response to call for aid from Gurkhas, 66th towards right & right centre. firing ceased 6.15 pm	
	9.15 pm	7th fired on trenches in front of Gurkhas who were attacked 66th also fired	
	6.15 pm	66th Battery shelled "white house" (x) also towards LA QUINQUE RUE (x	
7-11-14	3 am	7th Battery cooperated in repulse of attack from BOIS DE BIEZ ~~line~~ opposite 2/39 ~~Garhwal~~ Gharwal Rifles	
	6am	7th & 66th Batteries fired on trenches on left & left centre of 20th Infantry Bde. where heavy attack took place	
	9.15.	7th & 14th Batteries fired on German trenches & digging parties in front 1/39 Garhwal Rifles. This was repeated at 9.30 & 10.30 trenches in front of Seaforths being also shelled	
	6.15 pm	14th Battery shelled trenches near Bois du Biez	
	10.45 pm	7th, 14th & 37 Howitzer batteries cooperated in repulse of severe attack on right of 19th Infantry Brigade in front of Seaforths.	
8-11-14	1.30 am and 4.45 am	7th Battery opened fire on German attacks which were repulsed	

Gulab Singh & Sons, Calcutta—No. 22 Army C.—5-8-14—1,07,000.

Army Form C. 2118.

Instructions regarding War Diaries and Intelligence Summaries are contained in F. S. Regs., Part II, and the Staff Manual respectively. Title pages will be prepared in manuscript.

WAR DIARY
or
INTELLIGENCE SUMMARY.

(Erase heading not required.)

Hour, Date, Place.		Summary of Events and Information.	Remarks and references to Appendices.
8/11/14	11-5 am	37th Battery shelled NEUVE CHAPELLE with lyddite [illegible] has [illegible] at 11-30 am	At 1-45 pm [illegible] 14th Battery RFA [illegible] by rifle bullet [illegible] observing [illegible] RUE DU BOIS [illegible]
	12.5 [illegible]	37th Battery shelled new German works near LA QUINQUE RUE	
		66th Battery brought one section into action 400 yards E of the Rue [illegible] farm house	
9-11-14	10.15 am	7th & 14th shelled enemy's battery just SE of BOIS DE BIEZ also red gabled house a German observation post	
	10 [illegible]	Section 66th Bty shelled ground in front of salient near [illegible]	[illegible] 2/39
	11 10 am	37th Battery fired on German guns SE & E of BOIS DU BIEZ	
	11-30	" " " " Distillery (G) & houses [illegible]	
	3.30 pm 7.30 pm	" " " " German trenches near LA QUINQUE RUE	
	8.15 pm		
	10 - am	66th Battery shelled German battery east of BOIS DU BIEZ trenches W of Bois du Biez	
	4 pm ~~to 11 15 am~~		
	9.15 & 11-15 am	7th Battery fired a few shells at German infantry digging in front of 2/39 Garhwalis	
10/11/14	12 midnight	7th 14th & 37th formed in a heavy bombardment of the BOIS DU BIEZ firing 120 shrapnel 18 pr each (7 & 14) & 80 lyddite 37th Bty. Firing ceased 12 45 am	

Gulab Singh & Sons, Calcutta—No. 22 Army C.—5-8-14—1,07,000.

Instructions regarding War Diaries and Intelligence Summaries are contained in F. S. Regs., Part II, and the Staff Manual respectively. Title pages will be prepared in manuscript.

WAR DIARY

or

INTELLIGENCE SUMMARY.

(Erase heading not required.)

Army Form C. 2118.

Hour, Date, Place.	Summary of Events and Information.	Remarks and references to Appendices.
10 – 11 – 14. 3.26 am	37th How. Battery fired 10 rounds at new German trench	
10 am	7th Bty fired on enemy in front of 1/39	
9.45 am	37th Battery fired on German working parties near LAQUENQUE RUE	
* 11 – 11 – 14 – 12-to 12.45 am	Night Bombardment of BOIS DU BOIS. 7. 14. 37th batteries cooperated	
3. pm	7th Battery shelled enemys battery just E of QUINQUE RUE	
12 – 11 – 14 9.30 – 9.45	7th Battery shelled a Seve[?] gun battery 800x East of the WHITE HOUSE & silenced it the flashes were visible	
12.40 –	7th Battery engaged another battery in front of the left centre (1/39 Garhwalis) trenches	
12.30 – 1 pm	14th Battery shelled enemys battery flashes visible due east towards FE du BIE.	
4 pm – 4.35 pm	At 4 pm & 4.35 pm 14th Battery shelled German trenches in front of 1/39 & 2/39 Garhwalis.	
13 – 11 14 8 am	One Section 66th Battery shelled German trenches in front of 2/39 Garhwalis & S.W. of BOIS DE BIEZ. the 7th & 14 Batteries engaged the same target	20th Indian Infantry Brigade now called The GARHWAL BDE
9. PM	The 4th Bde & 65th Battery cooperated with the Garhwal Brigade in an attack on the German trenches immediately in front of the	

Gulab Singh & Sons, Calcutta—No. 22 Army C.—5-8-14—1,07,000.

Instructions regarding War Diaries and Intelligence Summaries are contained in F. S. Regs., Part II, and the Staff Manual respectively. Title pages will be prepared in manuscript.

WAR DIARY

or

INTELLIGENCE SUMMARY.

(Erase heading not required.)

Army Form C. 2118.

Hour, Date, Place.	Summary of Events and Information.	Remarks and references to Appendices.
13-11-14	junction of the 1/39 + 2/39 trenches. The infantry assault party started at 9 pm & at 9-5 pm was supported by rapid bursts of fire from all these batteries on German trenches bordering on them. The 65th Battery fired throughout the operation on the German trench to the right of the one assaulted by our infantry & enfiladed [?] trenches. The 7th Battery during the first 10 minutes shelled the same trench with rapid bursts of fire & at 9.15 searched to further area stretching up to the WHITE HOUSE & also further southwards. The 14th Battery throughout fired on a trench some 400 yards to the left front of the one assaulted in bursts of rapid fire from 9.5 to 9.15 pm & then in desultory manner. The 66th fired throughout on the German trenches to East of the LA BASSEE ROAD & SE of the corner LA BASSEE – RUE DU BOIS ROAD, first in bursts of fire from 9.5 pm to 9.15 pm & then in desultory fire.	
12 mn	At 12 midnight all batteries poured in rapid bursts of fire for 10 minutes in support of retirement of assaulting & working parties. The 7 & 14th then continued at moderate rate of fire till ordered to stop.	
14-11-14 8.30	The 65th Battery (attached whilst 37th resting) shelled trenches in front of our left centre.	

Gulab Singh & Sons, Calcutta—No. 22 Army C.—5-8-14—1,07,000.

Instructions regarding War Diaries and Intelligence Summaries are contained in F. S. Regs., Part II, and the Staff Manual respectively. Title pages will be prepared in manuscript.

WAR DIARY

or

INTELLIGENCE SUMMARY.

(Erase heading not required.)

Army Form C. 2118.

Hour, Date, Place.	Summary of Events and Information.	Remarks and references to Appendices.
15. 11·14. 5am	All batteries shelled the same trenches as last night in front	
	of Garhwal trenches & 2/3rd Gurkha Rifles.	
5·30	One section 66th Battery under Lieut Martin came under shell fire from	
	Enemys howitzer. Gr George Old was wounded in the thigh by a piece	
	of Base of HE shell. One gun was also hit but undamaged	
16 - 11 - 14	The 14th Battery fired on enemy sniping their observation post	
12·45	The 14th shelled enemys battery 86 & 25 east & west of LABASSEE Road	
3·45 pm	The 7th battery also engaged 8(a) near the same place as 86 & opposite	
	1/39 2/39 Garhwalis. The 37th Battery who had returned after 3 days	
	refitting verified lines at 10·40.	
1·35 – 2·10	37th Bty engaged enemys guns W of RUE DU MARAIS and No 25 as	
	above at 4·8 pm	
9 pm – 4·15	7th Battery shelled trenches at QUINQUE RUE & at 11·30 pm shelled	19th Bde now called DEHRA DUN Bde
	trenches in front of 1/39, 2/39 where a German attack took place	20th Bde now GARHWAL BDE
5·15 pm	14th Battery shelled enemy in front of DEHRA DUN BDE	21st Bde " BAREILLY BDE
9 pm	At 9 pm opened slow fire as though attack was threatened on trenches near	
9·25 pm	1/39, 2/39 junction & at 9·25 replied to enemys rifle fire on left of GARHWAL	
9·40 –	BDE. At 9·40 turned fire onto a searchlight seen on LABASSEE–	
	ROUGECROIX Road & swept up & down road but light disappeared	
6 pm	37th Battery shelled trenches in front of LEICESTERS on our right	
	trenches.	
17 – 11 – 14. 11 AM	7th Battery shelled trenches in front of 1/39 where Germans were	
	digging. At 4·5 pm to 6 pm shelled German diggers & at night shelled	
	a searchlight	

Gulab Singh & Sons, Calcutta—No. 22 Army C.—5-8-14—1,07,000.

Army Form C. 2118.

WAR DIARY

or

INTELLIGENCE SUMMARY.

(*Erase heading not required.*)

Instructions regarding War Diaries and Intelligence Summaries are contained in F. S. Regs., Part II, and the Staff Manual respectively. Title pages will be prepared in manuscript.

Hour, Date, Place.	Summary of Events and Information.	Remarks and references to Appendices.

Gulab Singh & Sons, Calcutta—No. 22 Army C.—5-8-14—1,07,000.

Army Form C. 2118.

Instructions regarding War Diaries and Intelligence Summaries are contained in F. S. Regs., Part II, and the Staff Manual respectively. Title pages will be prepared in manuscript.

WAR DIARY

or

INTELLIGENCE SUMMARY.

(Erase heading not required.)

Hour, Date, Place.		Summary of Events and Information.	Remarks and references to Appendices.
22-11-14		During day 7th Battery shelled two houses said to be enemy's observation houses on our left front.	
	3 pm	The 14th Battery shelled same houses which are 1 mile SW of BOIS DE BIEZ on LA BASSEE Road, fire was then turned onto BC's another observation house for enemy battery 25.* A man of 7th Battery was slightly wounded in arm by a stray German bullet.	*The 14th Battery again fired on houses 1 mile SW of BOIS DE BIEZ & after a few rounds the observation officer report them to be in flames & destroyed.
22-11-14	3 pm	7th Battery shelled enemy firing on left front & at 10.40 pm assisted in repelling an attack on left front	
23.11-14	9.50 am	7th shelled enemy's observation station at cross roads SW. of BOIS DE BIEZ	
	4.30 p	Fire was turned onto trenches on left front and southwards as far as RUE D'OUVERT to support a counter attack by BAREILLY BDE who had been partly pushed back about 2-20 pm. The counter attack did not succeed &	
	2.40 pm	14th Battery fired on observation house etc but mist came up & it was impossible to observe. At 4.30 pm the battery cooperated in a counter attack by Bareilly Bde to regain some lost ground. The fire extended in the ~~line~~ direction RUE DU MARAIS	
23.11.14	4.20 pm	which area was thoroughly searched with burst of 2 or 4 rounds.	
24.11.14.	12.30 am	The 7th Battery opened fire in support of a counter attack on ~~our~~ right of BAREILLY Bde. The counter attack on centre of BAREILLY BDE was renewed & the 7th Battery	
5.30-6.am	~~4.30 am~~	opened fire in support firing burst of rapid fire till the attack succeeded. 66th Battery relieved 7th at 7.3 am & at 12.3 pm shelled an enemy's observation house on LA BASSEE ROAD	
25/11/14	10.55 am	14th Battery located 4 emplacements to SE & ranged on them at 10.55 the occupants were soon seen to leave the emplacements were near the enemy battery 25 which was located SE of LA BASSEE ROAD range 3850	89 B14C

Gulab Singh & Sons, Calcutta—No. 22 Army C.—5-8-14—1,07,000.

Instructions regarding War Diaries and Intelligence Summaries are contained in F. S. Regs., Part II, and the Staff Manual respectively. Title pages will be prepared in manuscript.

WAR DIARY

or

INTELLIGENCE SUMMARY.

(Erase heading not required.)

Army Form C. 2118.

Hour, Date, Place.	Summary of Events and Information.	Remarks and references to Appendices.
25 – 11 – 14. 2.50 pm	14th Battery shelled enemy's observation house SE of LA BASSEE ROAD getting a direct hit. The 66th Battery shelled enemy sapping on left front & WHITE HOUSE. The occupants bolted hurriedly & no more digging occurred during daylight.	
3.50 pm	66th Bty opened on enemy attacking the left section of our front, the attack soon ceased.	
26 – 11 – 14	14th & 66th Btts shelled enemy digging in the morning in front of No 4 section. At midnight 66 & 14th fired for ½ hour in support of an attack near Rue [illegible]	JULLUNDUR BDE replaced GARHWAL BDE & front of Brigade is now divided into No 1, 2 3 & 4 Sections from South to North.
2.45 pm	~~Section~~ 66th Battery shelled enemy attacking No 4 section JULLUNDUR BD	
27 – 11 – 14 3 pm	14th Battery shelled an observation house & then searched for a battery opposite our left front.	
10.25 am	66th Battery shelled enemy sapping NW of plantation near BOIS DE BIEZ & stopped them working. At 2 pm the battery engaged enemy battery No 25 opposite No 2 section & afterwards shelled 2 observation houses.	
8 pm	Shelled enemy's trenches in front of No 3 section where heavy musketry fire had broken out, the musketry stopped at once.	
28 – 11 – 14 9.40 am	9.40 am ~~[illegible]~~ 14th Battery shelled enemy in the open retiring to their trenches.	
10.30 am	14th Bty shelled enemy's observation house which burst into flames [?]	
10.35 am	14th Bty shelled occupied house near cross roads SW of BOIS DE BIEZ fire appeared effective.	
3.20 pm	Fired at withdrawing infantry & 3.45 shelled observation house E [?] [illegible] & SE.	

Gulab Singh & Sons, Calcutta—No. 22 Army C.—5-8-14—1,07,000.

Instructions regarding War Diaries and Intelligence Summaries are contained in F. S. Regs., Part II, and the Staff Manual respectively. Title pages will be prepared in manuscript.

WAR DIARY
or
INTELLIGENCE SUMMARY.
(Erase heading not required.)

Army Form C. 2118.

Hour, Date, Place.	Summary of Events and Information.	Remarks and references to Appendices.
28-11-14. 7.30 AM	66th Battery RFA Observation officer saw Germans digging on the epaulments of battery 25 on which the battery had ranged the previous day. Four salvos were fired at a rapid rate. The 1st salvo was very effective & cleared the enemy who disappeared in a dip in the ground followed by 3 more salvos.	
12.30 pm	66th Battery stopped Germans working on a sap near plantation SW of Bois de Biez.	
11.30 am	7th Battery section in action near RUE DE BOIS shelled houses in front of No 2 section	
29-11-14.	14th Battery. Experimented with some H.E. 18 pdr shell (just received) on houses & trenches in front of No 4 section	
3.45 AM	Fired salvos at a trench near WHITE HOUSE which was seen to be occupied by the enemy.	
8.32 am	66th Battery shelled battery 25 & later experimented with HE shell at houses & trenches	Later reports state battery No 25 was effectively shelled out. This battery had at 8.30 fired on No 4 section & killed 2 & wounded 3.
30/11/14. 9.30 am	14th Battery shelled enemy's battery to SE. & at 11 AM shelled trenches in the same direction. Observation officer reported bullets	
11 am	falling in the trench which was partly enfiladed	
2.30 PM	Shelled enemy digging just north of above trench & enemy withdrew	

Gulab Singh & Sons, Calcutta—No. 22 Army C.—5-8-14—1,07,000.

Army Form C. 2118.

Instructions regarding War Diaries and Intelligence Summaries are contained in F. S. Regs., Part II, and the Staff Manual respectively. Title pages will be prepared in manuscript.

WAR DIARY

or

INTELLIGENCE SUMMARY.

(Erase heading not required.)

Hour, Date, Place.	Summary of Events and Information.	Remarks and references to Appendices.
30 – 11 – 14	66th Battery again shelled battery 26 [illegible] observing station.	The battery position here along the [illegible] CHAVATTES
	R.B. [illegible] Capt R.F.A. for O.C. 4th Bde R.F.A. 30-11-14	

Gulab Singh & Sons, Calcutta—No. 22 Army C.—5-8-14—1,07,000.

Meerut

A 2

War Diary
of
Headquarters 4th Bde R.F.A.

From 1-12-14
To 31-12-14

121/4046

Volume ___

Pp — to —

Army Form C. 2118.

WAR DIARY
or
INTELLIGENCE SUMMARY.

(Erase heading not required.)

Instructions regarding War Diaries and Intelligence Summaries are contained in F. S. Regs., Part II, and the Staff Manual respectively. Title pages will be prepared in manuscript.

Hour, Date, Place.	Summary of Events and Information.	Remarks and references to Appendices.
1-12-14 8.30am 10.34am 2.22 10.40	The 14th battery shelled an observing house using high explosive & shrapnel. Shelled houses near Distillery & at 11.33 shelled another observing house. Fired on enemy's infantry emerging from a house on LA BASSEE ROAD. 66th Battery shelled enemy's battery No 25. Later shelled houses in same direction.	
2-12-14 3.45pm 1pm 1.30pm 3.30	14th Battery shelled observing house 8C also at other houses at 1 pm & 1.30 pm. fire appeared effective. 66th Battery shelled enemy's battery 25 and 40 also at 1.30 shelled an observation post in some haystack which was seen on fire. At 3.30 again shelled 25 which showed activity.	
3-12-14 9.30am 2.25pm 9.50am 10.40am 11.45	The enemy active in front of [illegible] section so 66th Battery shelled trenches in front of 57. This was repeated at 2.25pm. [illegible] again became active & was shelled by 66th Battery. 7th Battery ranged on an observation post near cross roads S.E. of BOIS DE BIEZ. The 7th Battery on enemy moving in trenches in front of WHITE HOUSE. At 11.45 7th Bty shelled enemy working [illegible] in front of WHITE HOUSE & at 12 noon fired on enemy's sharpshooters.	
4-12-14 12 noon	7th Battery located a German machine gun & shelled it. From 2 to 3 pm battery fired at intervals at enemy's sharpshooters & the wire [illegible] our infantry's loopholes.	

Gulab Singh & Sons, Calcutta—No. 22 Army C.—5-8-14—1,07,000.

Army Form C. 2118.

WAR DIARY
or
INTELLIGENCE SUMMARY.

(Erase heading not required.)

Instructions regarding **War** Diaries and Intelligence Summaries are contained in F. S. Regs., Part II, and the Staff Manual respectively. Title pages will be prepared in manuscript.

Hour, Date, Place.	Summary of Events and Information.	Remarks and references to Appendices.
4 - 12 - 14 6.30 am	The 66th Battery at 6.30 am shelled enemy's trenches in front of No 4 section. This fire was in cooperation with the siege battery.	
(late report 3/12/14) 3.30 Pm	The 66th Bty shelled observation post near No 25 battery 3/12/14	
10 am	No 25 battery opened fire which was replied to with effect by 66th.	
2.30 P	Shelled trenches again whereupon enemy's battery 25 opened fire. The 66th then searched for No 25 which ceased firing	
5 - 12 - 14 12 noon	7th Battery shelled target No 25 an enemy's battery. This was done in cooperation with a heavy battery. Observation very difficult owing to weather.	
12.30 Pm	66th Battery shelled enemy's battery No 25. In the afternoon the 66th battery was shelled by enemy battery which was not located	
6 - 12 - 14 8 am	The 7th Battery fired at enemy's sharpshooters in WHITE HOUSE and	
10 40 Am	at 10.40 turned fire on enemy who were firing at our observing party	
3 Pm	Activity evident in front of No 3 section & 7th Batty fired on trenches	
3.30 Pm	Germans were seen entering houses near cross roads ESTAIRES LA BASSEE & RUE DU BOIS ROADS. 7th Bty put 4 HE shell into the house & one at back	
3 Pm	66th Battery shelled trenches in front of No 4 section & also sharpshooters at WHITE HOUSE. The plantation was also shelled where much digging had taken place during night. This was repeated ~~at~~	
5.15	after dark. At 5.15 pm 66th shelled a German sap near Plantation	
7 . 12 . 14	No firing took place. The weather was wet & misty.	
8 . 12 . 14 1 Pm	7th Battery fired on enemy's battery No 40 & ~~at 3~~ 66th battery also shelled No 40. The fire appeared effective. In the forenoon 66th battery shelled enemy trenches in front of left centre, were parties were seen to be	
3.45	working. At 3.45 7th Battery also shelled trenches in same direction	

Gulab Singh & Sons, Calcutta—No. 22 Army C.—5-8-14—1,07,000.

Instructions regarding War Diaries and Intelligence Summaries are contained in F. S. Regs., Part II, and the Staff Manual respectively. Title pages will be prepared in manuscript.

WAR DIARY

or

INTELLIGENCE SUMMARY.

(Erase heading not required.)

Army Form C. 2118.

Hour, Date, Place.	Summary of Events and Information.	Remarks and references to Appendices.
8-12-14	7th Bty Fired at enemys search light seen on left front.	
7 PM	66th Battery about an hour after dusk fired a salvo at enemys battery No 40 *	* No 40 had been hit during day & it was hoped to get working parties on the damaged front.
9-12-14 11.15 AM	7th Fired a few rounds at WHITE HOUSE but weather was too misty for observation. 66th & 12th did not fire till evening when at 8.30 PM musketry fire broke out opposite No 1 Section & 66th Battery fired on enemy trenches where musketry was coming from.	
10-12-14 8.30 AM	The 7th Battery shelled an occupied house also a party of Germans in vicinity	
10.34 AM	The 7th Battery shelled the same houses again & another where Germans were seen on both occasions the houses were hit several times	
11.30 AM	The 7th Battery shelled WHITE HOUSE Barn & several direct hits were obtained though some of the shell seemed to go right through & burst beyond. At 10 PM 7th Bty fired 2 salvos at searchlight	
10 PM	The 66th Battery fired on trenches opposite No 1 Section & stopped enemys musketry fire. Very misty & wet	
11-12-14	Very misty & impossible to observe till 2 pm when both 7th & 66th Batteries shelled some haystacks in enemys lines suspected observation posts. 7th Bty fired on enemys sharpshooters in front of No 3 section	
3.3 PM		
12-12-14 11 AM	66th Battery shelled enemy seen digging near a German Bty No 25 & afterwards shelled a "few likely observation posts". At 2 pm 7th Battery shelled house	
2 pm	from which smoke was issuing east of LA BASSEE ESTAIRES road 5 shell hit	
3 PM	Saw several Germans near houses 5 shell hit the house	

Gulab Singh & Sons, Calcutta—No. 22 Army C.—5-8-14—1,07,000.

Army Form C. 2118.

WAR DIARY
or
INTELLIGENCE SUMMARY.
(Erase heading not required.)

Instructions regarding War Diaries and Intelligence Summaries are contained in F. S. Regs., Part II, and the Staff Manual respectively. Title pages will be prepared in manuscript.

Hour, Date, Place.		Summary of Events and Information.	Remarks and references to Appendices.
12. 12. 14	7 PM	66th Battery shelled enemy's trenches & stopped their musketry fire at once.	
13. 12. 14.	8.15 AM	Enemy's battery No 25 opened fire 66th replied & silenced it. Later the 66th fired 2 shell at some mounted men who at once disappeared	
	12 noon	at 12 noon 7th Battery located some Germans cooking & put a few shell into them. Lieut Kiddle 7th Bty from a high chimney observed enemy's battery 25 to be very deeply entrenched & No 40 apparently vacant also a certain amount of movement between FE-DE-BIE & LORGIES	
	6 pm	Heavy firing broke out in front of No 1 section & 7th & 66th batteries opened on German trenches till the musketry ceased.	
14. 12. 14	7.30 AM	The 7th Battery fired at enemy's trenches in front of sections II & III where smoke from cooking was visible. At 8 am shelled	
	8 am	a party of Germans in a garden and at 9 am enemy reported by observation officer moving on NEUVE CHAPELLE – LORGIES road in southerly direction also wagons. The road was shelled at the same time the left section was turned onto trenches opposite salient near BOIS de BIEZ	
	9 am	Soon afterwards Lt Kiddle observing from a high chimney was seen by the enemy and a heavy shell fire was opened by them on the chimney & observation post	
	At 12.20 PM	7th Battery fired on houses South of road junction LA BASSEE – RUE DE BOIS roads. At 3.30 pm 7th Battery again fired on trenches	
	3.30 PM	in front of No 3 section	

Gulab Singh & Sons, Calcutta—No. 22 Army C.—5-8-14—1,07,000.

Army Form C. 2118.

Instructions regarding War Diaries and Intelligence Summaries are contained in F. S. Regs., Part II, and the Staff Manual respectively. Title pages will be prepared in manuscript.

WAR DIARY

or

INTELLIGENCE SUMMARY.

(Erase heading not required.)

Hour, Date, Place.	Summary of Events and Information.	Remarks and references to Appendices.
14-12-14 9.10am	66th Battery shelled enemy's battery which had opened on Bareilly post, & later on German trenches.	
15-12-14	The 7th Battery observed (No 25) enemy's battery active & shelled it promptly.	
9.15am	At 9.15am enemy collected in red house in F2(b) shelled it.	
10.30am	(No 40) hostile battery opened fire & 7th Battery shelled & neutralized it.	
12.35p	Sharpshooters opposite left section GARHWAL Bde. apparent but were quieted with a few rounds, & at 3.30 signs of life were visible in an enclosure to SE which was shelled.	
9.40am	66th Battery – At 9.40am fired on an occupied house & obtained several direct hits. (No 40) Enemy's battery opened fire & 66 replied	
10.30a 11.0a	putting a percussion shrapnel into the emplacement. At 11 am again shelled (No 40) with high explosive & got one round well in.	
3.15p	66th scored several direct hits on occupied houses to SE	
9.53pm 10.35	66th shelled enemy planting wire entanglements & at 10.35 fired a few rounds at enemy in trenches due W. & opposite No 3 section	
16-12-14 6am	Both 7th & 66th batteries opened an irregular fire on the enemy's trenches in front of Garhwal Brigade. The 66th Battery then turned fire on No 25 in hopes of catching the detachment manning [illegible]	
7.30a	The 14th Battery opened fire from a new position near Croix BARBEE & registered zones 6 & 14.	

Gulab Singh & Sons, Calcutta—No. 22 Army C.—5-8-14—1,07,000.

Army Form C. 2118.

WAR DIARY

or

INTELLIGENCE SUMMARY.

(Erase heading not required.)

Instructions regarding War Diaries and Intelligence Summaries are contained in F. S. Regs., Part II, and the Staff Manual respectively. Title pages will be prepared in manuscript.

Hour, Date, Place.	Summary of Events and Information.	Remarks and references to Appendices.
16. 12. 14. 11 Am	at 11am a captive baloon appeared in the German lines in direction of LIGNY LE PETIT but was out of range. At 11.30 the 66th Bty	
11.30 Am	shelled LORGIES which showed signs of occupation. At 1.30 Pm	A blind shell found at O.P. was reported as follows
1.30	the 7th Battery began registering some trenches to S.E. but were interrupted by the Observation post being shelled. A tall Chimney near the observ. Post was knocked down	Calibre 15 centimetres length with fuze 42 centimetres. W inside small circle, only mark on base. Colour Red. weight 80 Kgs. lbs
9 Pm	The 66th Battery shelled enemy opposite left section who had been definitely located constructing wire entanglements	
17. 12. 14. 10.45	The 14th Battery noticed activity at the distillery & shelled it getting 4 direct hits. The 66th Batty also shelled it with the same	
11.15	result. At 11.15 the 7th Battery shelled some enemy's working parties near a German redoubt opposite Centre section	
2 Pm.	A hostile battery opened fire in a southerly direction & was enfiladed by 7th Battery, who silenced it, later our heavy ~~Battery~~ battery turned onto the same target & the 7th Bty fired a few rounds in cooperation. The 4th Bde was relieved by the 13th Bde during the afternoon & the 7th, 66th Batteries 4 Bde A.C. & H.Qrs marched to billets in rest at ROBECQ. The 14th Battery going to PARADIS	
18th to 25th	The Brigade remained in the same billets	

Gulab Singh & Sons, Calcutta—No. 22 Army C.—5-8-14—1,07,000.

Army Form C. 2118.

Instructions regarding War Diaries and Intelligence Summaries are contained in F. S. Regs., Part II, and the Staff Manual respectively. Title pages will be prepared in manuscript.

WAR DIARY
or
INTELLIGENCE SUMMARY.

(Erase heading not required.)

Hour, Date, Place.	Summary of Events and Information.	Remarks and references to Appendices.
26-12-14	The brigade moved to fresh billets at AMES and BELLERY S.E. of LILLERS.	
31-12-14.	Brigade still in rest at same billets	
	R B Martin Capt R.F.A. for O.C. 4th Bde R.F.A.	

Gulab Singh & Sons, Calcutta—No. 22 Army C.—5-8-14—1,07,000.

4th Bde
[illegible] 96

War Diary
of
7th Battery R. F. A
from 1-9-14
to 30-11-14
Pp 1 to 7
Volume I

WAR DIARY
or
INTELLIGENCE SUMMARY.
(Erase heading not required.)

Army Form C. 2118

1

Instructions regarding War Diaries and Intelligence Summaries are contained in F. S. Regs., Part II, and the Staff Manual respectively. Title pages will be prepared in manuscript.

7th Battery RFA

Hour, Date, Place.	Summary of Events and Information.	Remarks and references to Appendices
Trimulgherry. Deccan. India 1st Sept 1914	First day of Mobilization. ~~all orders & instructions~~ Steps taken to comply with all orders & instructions.	WMR
12th Sept 1914.	Received concentration orders.	
14th Sept 1914.	Entrained at SECUNDERABAD Stn. in two trains.	Still wanting to complete by 1 Capt. 2 Cpls. 1 Br. 8 Drivers. 15 horses.
15 Sept 1914	1st train left 0.55 AM. 2nd train 2.45 AM.	
16 Sept 1914 BOMBAY	1st train arrived BOMBAY. 6 AM. 2nd train 7.45 AM. Detrained & went into bivouac at CARNAL BUNDER, BB & CI. Goods Yard.	
17th Sept 1914.	1 horse destroyed incurably injured. 1 man to COLABA Hospital	Received 2 Cpls 1 Br. 8 drs. from 95 Bty. 15 horses from 96th Bty 1 horse " 95 "
19th Sept 1914.	Embarked on ~~H~~ Transport SUBADAR at PRINCESS DOCK.	10 joined from 96 Bty.
20th Sept. 1914. about 12. noon	Sailed from BOMBAY along with 28 other transports & escort	[illegible]
14th Oct 1914	Arrived Marseilles commenced disembarkation	
15th "	Completed disembarkation & marched to camp at Parc Borély Marseilles	
17th "	Entrained at St Charles Station during night	
18th "	Left Marseilles about 6 AM.	
20th "	Arrived Orleans & camped at Les Groues	

WMR

Gulab Singh & Sons, Calcutta—No. 22 Army C.—5-8-14—1,07,000.

Instructions regarding War Diaries and Intelligence Summaries are contained in F. S. Regs., Part II, and the Staff Manual respectively. Title pages will be prepared in manuscript.

WAR DIARY

or

INTELLIGENCE SUMMARY. 7th Battery RFA

(*Erase heading not required.*)

Army Form C. 2118. 2.

Hour, Date, Place.	Summary of Events and Information.	Remarks and references to Appendices.
27th October 1914	Left Orleans at 8.15 PM.	WKKR
29 " "	Arrived LILLERS at 7.40 AM. detrained & marched to MIRVILLE where Bty was billeted.	WKKR
30th October	Marched to Le FASSONS 8 miles.	WKKR See sketch I WKKR
31st "	Brigade relieved 27th Bde RFA of 5th Div in trenches 7th Bty in reserve went into bivouac at (A) was located by German aeroplane which dropped bombs without effect. Afterwards a couple of heavy shell fell over Bty.	" " "
1st Nov.	Still in reserve. Moved back to bivouac at LA TOURET	WKKR WKKR
2nd Nov near RICHBOURG St VAAST	Relieved 66th Bty entrenched at (B) in sketch. Fired now & then on German trenches range 2200x our own Infy being about 150 to 200 yds from them.	Country is about as bad as could be for artillery work. Being flat, cultivated & much enclosed. Observation extremely difficult & only possible by having forward observing stations. WKKR

Gulab Singh & Sons, Calcutta—No. 22 Army C.—5-8-14—1,07,000.

Army Form C. 2118. (3

Instructions regarding War Diaries and Intelligence Summaries are contained in F. S. Regs., Part II, and the Staff Manual respectively. Title pages will be prepared in manuscript.

WAR DIARY
or
INTELLIGENCE SUMMARY.
(Erase heading not required.)

7th Battery RGA

Hour, Date, Place.	Summary of Events and Information.	Remarks and references to Appendices.
3rd November Marten near RICHEBOURG St VAAST	Little doing during the day. Germans attacked 1/39 GHARWAL Rifles whose trenches are to our immediate front. As we had previously verified range & line to German trenches we opened fire. ~~[illegible]~~ The attack was repulsed. Received thanks of OC 1/39 GR for our support the fire was most effective.	Weather damp, raw cold. Generally misty in morning. Some sunshine. WMcR
4th Nov.	Desultory fighting all around. In afternoon 19th Infy Bde were attacked. Tried to cooperate (on our left) by getting line & range from maps. Observation impossible. 1/39 GR again attacked at night. Cooperated effectively.	WMcR
5th Nov.	Attack during day on 21st Infy Bde on our right tried to cooperate, getting line & range from maps. Night attack on 1/39 GR as usual	WMcR

Gulab Singh & Sons, Calcutta—No. 22 Army C.—5-8-14—1,07,000.

Army Form C. 2118. (4

Instructions regarding War Diaries and Intelligence Summaries are contained in F. S. Regs., Part II, and the Staff Manual respectively. Title pages will be prepared in manuscript.

WAR DIARY
or
INTELLIGENCE SUMMARY.

7th Battery R.F.A.

(Erase heading not required.)

Hour, Date, Place.	Summary of Events and Information.	Remarks and references to Appendices.
6th Nov	Desultory fighting night & day.	WKKR
7th Nov	Same. during night attack B.G. was sniped went out with party to try & locate snipers but could find nothing.	WKKR
8th Nov.	Same. except no night attack.	Horses develope pink eye. WKKR
9th Nov. 8.30 PM.	Same. 1/39 G.R. attacked & drove the Germans out of trench about 150x to their front Germans surprised, B.G. cooperated & by fire to prevent reinforcements coming up from other German trenches. various shakes in front during the night, B.G. fired a few rounds at German trenches when these were on & German rifle fire then stopped. B.G. sniped during most of the time evidently snipers fired at flashes of guns. Party sent out but could not find any of them.	WKKR
		WKKR

Gulab Singh & Sons, Calcutta—No. 22 Army C.—5-8-14—1,07,000.

Instructions regarding War Diaries and Intelligence Summaries are contained in F. S. Regs., Part II, and the Staff Manual respectively. Title pages will be prepared in manuscript.

WAR DIARY
or
INTELLIGENCE SUMMARY.

(Erase heading not required.)

Army Form C. 2118.

7th Bgde RFA

Hour, Date, Place.	Summary of Events and Information.	Remarks and references to Appendices.
10th Nov.	Usual intermittent firing during the day. As reports had been received that enemy were collecting in & about BOIS DU BIEZ, a number of Batteries were told off to fire at midnight for 3/4 of an hour on the locality in question.	WKR
11th Nov.	From forward observing station some of enemys guns were located & shelled, evidently with some effect for they stopped firing. No night attack.	A high wind, cold & some rain. WKR
12th Nov.	Fired on two of enemys batteries that had been located.	High wind, more or less dry & some sunshine. WKR
13th Nov. 9 PM.	~~9 PM~~ # Detachments of 1/39 2/39 GARHWAL Rifles & 2/3 Gurkhas attacked trench of Germans 50 yds to their front. All Batteries in vicinity cooperated, in attack & afterwards when it was found impracticable to destroy trench ## the retirement & removal of wounded was covered by fire from 7 & 14" Batteries which continued firing at intervals till 5 AM on 14th Nov.	# Cold, wet & high wind. WKR

Gulab Singh & Sons, Calcutta—No. 22 Army C.—5-8-14—1,07,000.

Instructions regarding War Diaries and Intelligence Summaries are contained in F. S. Regs., Part II, and the Staff Manual respectively. Title pages will be prepared in manuscript.

WAR DIARY

or

INTELLIGENCE SUMMARY.

(Erase heading not required.)

Army Form C. 2118.

7 Bty RFA

(6

Hour, Date, Place.	Summary of Events and Information.	Remarks and references to Appendices.
14th Nov.	Not much doing as regards 7 Bty.	Cold wet windy WMcK
15th "	" " " "	Frost, sleet, rain, & gale blowing. WMcK
16 "	" " " "	
17th "	" " " " shelling snipers who were worrying our infantry also diggers who showed signs of activity in enemy's trenches.	" " WMcK
		WMcK
18 "	" " "	hard frost. bright sun for a good part of day. WMcK
19 "	Not much doing. desultory sniping & shelling going on. (whenever there is infantry fight in front or on left a lot of rifle bullets come over & into the Battery.)	frost in morning, snow in afternoon WMcK
20.	" " " " "	ground white with snow Temp in shade 9 AM. 20° F WMcK
21st "	" " " " "	Temp. 8 AM. 20° F. WMcK
22nd "	" " " " " about 5 PM Infantry firing on left front. 1 man wounded in arm by rifle bullet from enemy's trenches.	" " WMcK

Instructions regarding War Diaries and Intelligence Summaries are contained in F. S. Regs., Part II, and the Staff Manual respectively. Title pages will be prepared in manuscript.

Army Form C. 2118.

WAR DIARY
or
INTELLIGENCE SUMMARY.
(*Erase heading not required.*)

7th Bde R.F.A.

Hour, Date, Place.		Summary of Events and Information.	Remarks and references to Appendices.
In action near RICHEBOURG St VAAST. 23rd Nov.	4 PM.	received information that BAREILLY Bde had been forced back in centre, & that counterattack was to be made at 4:30 AM. when Bty was to cooperate as far as possible by firing on enemy lines in that direction. This was near our S limit of fire, & owing to danger of firing on our own trenches, Bty could only cooperate by firing in direction where one might suppose enemies supports & reserves might be. Fired about 70 rounds until sound of fight ceased.	Temperature 8 AM. 17° F [initials]
24th Nov.	12 MN.	Was informed another counterattack was to be made but no time specified.	
	5:30 AM.	Heavy firing in direction of BAREILLY Bde [illegible] for short time.	[initials]
	6 AM.	" " " "	[initials]
	8 AM.	66th Bde RFA arrived & relieved 7th Bde which went into reserve at LE TOURET, having been in action night and day since 2nd Nov.	Much difficulty in moving guns owing to ice on roads. Thaw set in during course of day. [illegible] accordingly. [initials]
25th Nov.		In reserve. MEERUT Divn has now been relieved by LAHORE Divn & 4th Bde RFA which still remain at front comes under C.R.A. of Latter.	[initials]
26th 27th 28th 29th 30th		Still in reserve nothing doing.	[initials]

Gulab Singh & Sons, Calcutta—No. 22 Army C.—5-8-14—1,07,000.

War diary. 7 Bg RFA

Sketch I

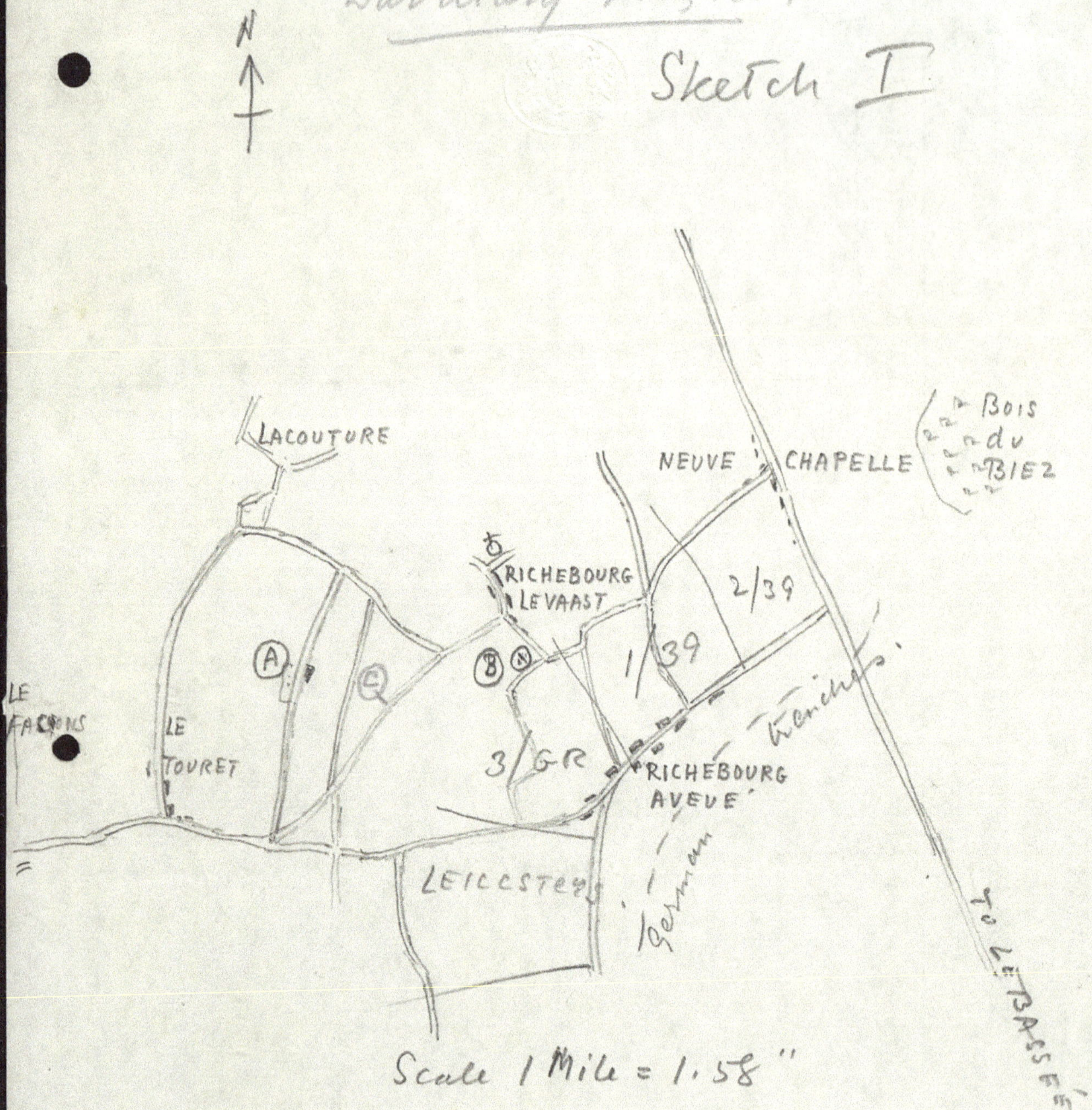

N

LACOUTURE

NEUVE CHAPELLE

Bois du BIEZ

RICHEBOURG LEVAAST

2/39

1/39

A

C

B

LE FACONS

LE TOURET

3/GR

RICHEBOURG AVEUE

German trenches

LEICESTERS

To LA BASSEE

Scale 1 Mile = 1.58"

WKR

[illegible] [illegible]ally. 18-4

31.3 [illegible]

Army Form C. 2118.

WAR DIARY
66 Battery R F A
or
INTELLIGENCE ~~SUMMARY.~~
(*Erase heading not required.*)

Instructions regarding War Diaries and Intelligence Summaries are contained in F. S. Regs., Part II, and the Staff Manual respectively. Title pages will be prepared in manuscript.

Hour, Date, Place.	Summary of Events and Information.	Remarks and references to Appendices.
1914		
August 31	Ordered to Mobilize.	
September 15	Battery left Secunderabad in two trains for Bombay.	
" 16	Arrived in Bombay	
" 17	Detrained and bivouacked in Carnac Bunder Goods Yard (BB&CI Railway)	
" 19	Embarked with Brigade Staff on HT TAROBA.	
	Strength of Battery Officers 4 NCO's & men 171 Native Drivers 10 " Shoeing Smiths 2 Private Followers 8	

Gulab Singh & Sons. Calcutta—No. 22 Army C.—5 8 14—1,07,000.

Instructions regarding War Diaries and Intelligence Summaries are contained in F. S. Regs., Part II, and the Staff Manual respectively. Title pages will be prepared in manuscript.

WAR DIARY
or
INTELLIGENCE SUMMARY.
(Erase heading not required.)

Army Form C. 2118.

2

Hour, Date, Place.	Summary of Events and Information.	Remarks and references to Appendices.
1914	Horses 178.	
September 20	H T TAROBA left Bombay 11 a m with convoy under escort.	
" 24	Horse Army Number 1611, Battery No 101 died during night from heat apoplexy.	
October 3	Arrived Suez at 6 a m. Took on board 159 Sacks Bran and 18 Sacks Barley.	
" 4	Arrived Port Said 4 30 p m. Took on board 92 Sacks Bran.	
" 7	Left Port Said with convoy under French Escort.	

Gulab Singh & Sons, Calcutta—No. 22 Arms C—5 8 14—1,07,000

Army Form C. 2118.

3

Instructions regarding War Diaries and Intelligence Summaries are contained in F. S. Regs., Part II, and the Staff Manual respectively. Title pages will be prepared in manuscript.

WAR DIARY
or
INTELLIGENCE SUMMARY.

66th Battery R.F.A.

(*Erase heading not required.*)

Hour, Date, Place.	Summary of Events and Information.	Remarks and references to Appendices.
October 14th	Arrived Marseilles at 4 pm. disembarked vehicles & mules & about 20 horses during night	
" 15th	Completed disembarkation, marched to Camp in Parc Borely, where Battery arrived about 4 pm.	
" 16	Exceptional heavy rain, whole camp under water.	
17.	Left Camp at Parc BORELY at 2.45 pm & bivouacked for night in Shed at Docks.	
18.	Entrained Battery; & train left for Orleans at 11 am.	
20	Arrived Orleans at 3 pm & marched to Camp where Battery arrived in dark at 7 pm.	

Gulab Singh & Sons, Calcutta —No. 22 Army C.—5 8 14—1,07,000.

A/

S. 1

121/4046

114th Battery R.F.A.

War Diary From 31 – 8 – 1914

To 4 – 1 – 1915

1

Instructions regarding War Diaries and Intelligence Summaries are contained in F. S. Regs., Part II, and the Staff Manual respectively. Title pages will be prepared in manuscript.

WAR DIARY

or

INTELLIGENCE SUMMARY.

(Erase heading not required.)

Army Form C. 2118

Hour, Date, Place.	Summary of Events and Information.	Remarks and references to Appendices
Secunderabad 31-8-14	Ordered to mobilize	
" 15-9-14	Left Secunderabad for Bombay (entrained)	
Bombay 16-9-14	Arrived	
" 19-9-14	Embarked per H.T. "Knight Companion" 14th B. R.F.A. part 9th Al R.F.A. part Indore Transport Coy	
" 20-9-14	Sailed	
At Sea	1 Horse died	
Port Suez 3-10-14	Arrived	
" " 5-10-14	Left	
Port Said 6-10-14	Arrived	
" 7-10-14	Left	

Army Form C. 2118.

WAR DIARY
or
INTELLIGENCE SUMMARY.
(*Erase heading not required.*)

Instructions regarding War Diaries and Intelligence Summaries are contained in F. S. Regs., Part II, and the Staff Manual respectively. Title pages will be prepared in manuscript.

Hour, Date, Place.		Summary of Events and Information.	Remarks and references to Appendices
Marseilles	14-10-14	Arrived	
"	15-10-14	Camped at Rue Marceau	
"	18-10-14	Entrained for Orleans	
Orleans	20-10-14	Arrived & camped at Les Groues	
		Halted at Orleans – received a certain amt. of deficient equipment replaced casualties. Capt Turnbull & Lieut Pollen reported for temp. duty in France.	
	27.10.14	Entrained at Orleans	
Merville	29.10.14	Detrained at Berguette marched into Merville (billets) 8 miles arrived 4.30 pm.	
Les Facons	30.10.14	Marched S.S.E to Les Facons (arr 4.30 pm) – arrangements made by C.R.A. Meerut to occupy positions now occupied by Batteries of 5th Division. 16th Battery to occupy position of 121st Battery near Rue des Chavattes (across map 1" = 1¼ mls)	
	31.	C.O. reconnoitred this position –	
Rue des Chavatte	31.10.14	Marched from Les Facons (0.30 am) to Rue des Chavattes (5 mls)	

Army Form C. 2118.

WAR DIARY

or

INTELLIGENCE SUMMARY.

(Erase heading not required.)

Instructions regarding War Diaries and Intelligence Summaries are contained in F. S. Regs., Part II, and the Staff Manual respectively. Title pages will be prepared in manuscript.

Hour, Date, Place.		Summary of Events and Information.	Remarks and references to Appendices
Rue des Chavattes	31.10.14 (contd)	and occupied a covered position fully entrenched & hidden from view of aeroplanes - an observation officer was sent forward about 1 mile S.E. of Battery position to houses on the Rue du Bois - lines laid out and all arrangements made for opening fire by 8.15 am. Telephone equipment supplied to Battery very inadequate + inferior - this being the only method of inter-communication possible in a country of this nature a better & fuller equipment should be ~~supplied~~ supplied. Opened fire on a German Infantry attack at 1.35 pm. from the direction of La Quinque Rue - result not known but attack apparently repulsed - Opened fire at 11.10 pm, at 11.30 pm., at 1.5 am. and at 5.15 am. to assist	
- do -	1.11.14	our Infantry in the trenches - result not known - More desultory shooting during the day but no definite target observed - Observation party had to desert their station twice during the day, driven out by heavy shell fire - no casualties. Held in readiness to move in evening, teams being brought up to gun line after dark, and new positions reconnoitred towards LE TOURET - No move carried out.	
- do -	2-11-14 6.45 am.	At dawn searched for 2 of the enemy's guns reported to be in front of 2/39th Garhwalis' trenches: as communication with	

Army Form C. 2118.

Instructions regarding War Diaries and Intelligence Summaries are contained in F. S. Regs., Part II, and the Staff Manual respectively. Title pages will be prepared in manuscript.

WAR DIARY

or

INTELLIGENCE SUMMARY.

(Erase heading not required.)

Hour, Date, Place.	Summary of Events and Information.	Remarks and references to Appendices
	this regiment was broken, no results could be obtained, but these guns were not reported as firing. More desultory shelling in direction of 'reported' guns, merely resulting in slight waste of ammunition.	
2.15 pm.	Shelled part of 3 Gurkha trenches during an attack made on this regiment (2.15 pm.): attack apparently repulsed. Observation Officer again shelled out of his post.	

Army Form C. 2118.

Instructions regarding War Diaries and Intelligence Summaries are contained in F. S. Regs., Part II, and the Staff Manual respectively. Title pages will be prepared in manuscript.

WAR DIARY
or
INTELLIGENCE SUMMARY.
(*Erase heading not required.*)

Hour, Date, Place.		Summary of Events and Information.	Remarks and references to Appendices
Les CHAVATTES	7.11.14 10.10 am.	Shelled German trenches during an attack on the 19th Infy Bde.	
	2.30 pm.	Some desultory shooting at supposed German observation stations	
	6.15 pm.	Another attack as at 10.10 am. - again shelled in same direction	
	11 pm.	ditto ditto.	
		Battery ordered to dig an alternative gun position near present one.	
- do -	8.11.14 10.55 am.	Shelled German observn. Station supposed to be in a House.	
		Continued preparing alternative position.	
	1.30 pm.	Lieut Pritchard slightly wounded by bullet at Observing Station.	
- do -	9.11.14 10.15 am.	Shelled position of 2 German Batteries - too misty for observation	
	11.15 am.	Shelled a presumed German observation station in a house - effect appeared good.	
- do -	10.11.14 12.15 pm.	Shelled German trenches facing those of 3rd Gurkhas at a range of about 3000x.	
	12.52 pm.	Fired on large supporting trench, 500x in rear of above trench. range found but -	
	11.11.14 12 midnight - 12.45 am	Searched and swept area of the BOIS DU BIEZ and ground E of that wood in conjunction with the other Batteries of the Divn.	

Army Form C. 2118.

Instructions regarding War Diaries and Intelligence Summaries are contained in F. S. Regs., Part II, and the Staff Manual respectively. Title pages will be prepared in manuscript.

WAR DIARY

or

INTELLIGENCE SUMMARY.

(Erase heading not required.)

Hour, Date, Place.	Summary of Events and Information.	Remarks and references to Appendices
LES CHAVATTES 11-11-14	No shelling all day.	
do 12.11.14 ~~4pm~~ 12.30pm – 1pm	Shelled flashes of enemy's guns in direction of LIGNY LE PETIT (5750ˣ) : shooting appeared effective – C.F. 1pm.	
4pm	Ranged on German trenches facing position of 1st & 2nd 39th Garhwal[illegible] trenches – close in front of latter.	
4.35pm	Rapid bursts of fire on above trenches – according to Obs Officer fire seemed effective	
4.45pm	Ceased firing	
– do – 13.11.14 8am	Fire on German trenches SE of the BOIS DU BIEZ – 20 rounds.	
8.8am	Ceased firing – Effect unable to be observed.	
– do – night of 13-11-14 / 14-11-14 9pm	Commenced shelling supporting German trenches almost due E trench[illegible] on left of 2 Gurkhas [illegible] fill in an advanced German trench. Steady bursts of fire at first & then a slow rate until midnight when bursts were	
do 14.11.14 12 mn	renewed – from 12.30am till 5am maintained a slow fire on same	
5am	area. Ceased firing at 5.17am. Fired about 260 rounds.	
– do – 15.11.14 5am	Slight shelling only at 5am in anticipation of an attack which did not materialize.	
– do – 16.11.14	Desultory shelling during the day : nothing of importance. [illegible]	

Army Form C. 2118.

WAR DIARY
or
INTELLIGENCE SUMMARY.
(Erase heading not required.)

Instructions regarding War Diaries and Intelligence Summaries are contained in F. S. Regs., Part II, and the Staff Manual respectively. Title pages will be prepared in manuscript.

Hour, Date, Place.	Summary of Events and Information.	Remarks and references to Appendices
LES CHAVATTES 16.11.14 5pm	Was warned of an attack being made on right flank of 19 Infantry Brigade, I turned fire of Battery on trenches SW of the BOIS DU BIEZ and northwards to help in meeting this attack - Similarly	
9.30pm	at 9.30 pm and also turned a section on to a searchlight reported on the LA BASSEE Road - Ceased firing at 9.55pm.	
do 17.11.14 8.30am	Shelled Germans digging trenches near LA BASSEE road in square B10c (map 142 H) - only fired a few shells - desultory shooting during the day - Shelled a German searchlight	
11pm	about 11 pm. Effect unknown, probably nil - Heard of Lord Roberts' death -	
do - 18.11.14 5.40 pm.	Shelled enemy's supporting trenches on hearing heavy Infy fire on left flank of Garhwal Infy Bde - very short attack -	
11.20pm	Shelled German trenches opposite 2nd Gurkhas - only a few rounds	
do 19.11.14 7am	Occupied alternative position owing to muddy condition of first posn.	
10-12am	Checked lines of fire	
2pm	Heavy snow nothing doing -	

Army Form C. 2118.

WAR DIARY

or

INTELLIGENCE SUMMARY.

(Erase heading not required.)

Instructions regarding War Diaries and Intelligence Summaries are contained in F. S. Regs., Part II, and the Staff Manual respectively. Title pages will be prepared in manuscript.

Hour, Date, Place.	Summary of Events and Information.	Remarks and references to Appendices

Army Form C. 2118.

Instructions regarding War Diaries and Intelligence Summaries are contained in F. S. Regs., Part II, and the Staff Manual respectively. Title pages will be prepared in manuscript.

WAR DIARY

or

INTELLIGENCE SUMMARY.

(Erase heading not required.)

Hour, Date, Place.			Summary of Events and Information.	Remarks and references to Appendices
LES CHAVATTES	23.11.14	11.32 am	At 11.32 fired at flashes of guns about 5° right of Cross roads only fired a few rds as observn was very difficult	
		11.46 am 11.51 am	Resumed shelling house at X roads – reported house destroyed in flames. Ceased at 11.51 am	
		2.40 pm	Shelled a house (8c) but very misty for observn.	
		4.20 pm	Received information that BAREILLY Infy Bde were to try & recover some ground lost during the day at dusk and that the Battery was to co-operate as far South as the RUE D'OUVERT	
		4.32 pm	(142 J – B1c+d) – At 4.32 pm searched area of the RUE DU MARAIS (142 F5d) with ranges varying from 4000 to 3600 yds –	
		5.8 pm	Employed bursts of fire – about 60 rds – CF 5.8 pm.	
			N.B. Might have lowered range, but owing to complaints by Infy of shell falling near their trenches from our Batteries, did not like doing so –	
"	24.11.14		Blank day as reported shortly. LAHORE DIVN relieved the MEERUT DIVN.	
"	25.11.14	10.55 am	Ranged on new emplacements being made (142 B14c) and	

Army Form C. 2118.

Instructions regarding War Diaries and Intelligence Summaries are contained in F. S. Regs., Part II, and the Staff Manual respectively. Title pages will be prepared in manuscript.

WAR DIARY

or

INTELLIGENCE SUMMARY.

(Erase heading not required.)

Hour, Date, Place.	Summary of Events and Information.	Remarks and references to Appendices

1

Instructions regarding War Diaries and Intelligence Summaries are contained in F. S. Regs., Part II, and the Staff Manual respectively. Title pages will be prepared in manuscript.

WAR DIARY
or
INTELLIGENCE SUMMARY.
(*Erase heading not required.*)

Army Form C. 2118.

Hour, Date, Place.		Summary of Events and Information.	Remarks and references to Appendices
LES CHATTES	28/11/14 (continued) 10.32 am	Turned fire another house S of P.t F. occupied by the enemy – this seemed effective –	
– do –	3.20 pm	Shelled withdrawing Infantry & an old observation house (called 8C) – Stopped at 4. pm.	
		Heard of Russians being victorious in big battle near LODZ.	
– do –	29/11/14 9.30 am – 11.30 am	Carried out comparison of H.E. Shell with Shrapnel. The latter ranges slightly further at long range: and did not always detonate properly, & some blind in the heavy ploughed field. Shrapnel almost as good for observ^n purposes. Fired at (1) a house with a corrector (2) percussion at a house (3) perch at a trench. A corrector of 162 required. Ranges varied from 4000^x to 3200^x.	
do	3.45 pm	Fired salvoes at a trench in Sq B 13 d (1422) seen to be occupied by enemy. Fire reported apparently effective.	
– do –	30/11/14 9.30 am	Fired salvoes at flashes of a gun, presumed to have been ranged on before. Fire however not effective as though in some time the enemy gun (or guns) had been moved further back.	

Army Form C. 2118.

WAR DIARY

or

INTELLIGENCE SUMMARY.

(Erase heading not required.)

Instructions regarding War Diaries and Intelligence Summaries are contained in F. S. Regs., Part II, and the Staff Manual respectively. Title pages will be prepared in manuscript.

Hour, Date, Place.	Summary of Events and Information.	Remarks and references to Appendices

1

Army Form C. 2118.

WAR DIARY

or

INTELLIGENCE SUMMARY.

(Erase heading not required.)

Instructions regarding War Diaries and Intelligence Summaries are contained in F. S. Regs., Part II, and the Staff Manual respectively. Title pages will be prepared in manuscript.

Hour, Date, Place.		Summary of Events and Information.	Remarks and references to Appendices
LES CHAVATTES	2/12/14 (cont) 3.45pm	Shelled enemy's observ. house in Square F 26 (142 h) Range 4675 yds got direct hits. - the fire seemed effective -	
	3/12/14 8 am	Relieved in present position by 7th Battery R.F.A. who took over most of our telephone equipment - again this equipment seems very bad + too little supplied of it. One section 14th Battery relieved section of 7th Battery in action near Cse DU RUILX (E 1 a 142 h) at same time. This section is apparently necessary to provide a certain emplacement fire along the trenches in the direction of NEUVE CHAPELLE (B 6 b 142 h) - apparently chiefly for night work + only in one fixed direction - Remainder of Battery withdrew into billets near LE TOURET - A certain amount of pink-eye (influenza) still among horses but not of the same virulent type that appeared 3 weeks ago - their temperature not so high and they do not fall away so quickly - 3 or 4 cases of sores in corner of mouth (like bit injuries), difficult to diagnose, probably poisoned by nibbling some native of tree - Vety Officer cannot diagnose either. Segregate these as well as the pinkeye cases. Billet dirty + crowded, natives and Europeans mixed together - the natives (mule corps) being out of all control as regards sanitation -	

Army Form C. 2118.

WAR DIARY

or

INTELLIGENCE SUMMARY.

(Erase heading not required.)

Instructions regarding War Diaries and Intelligence Summaries are contained in F. S. Regs., Part II, and the Staff Manual respectively. Title pages will be prepared in manuscript.

Hour, Date, Place.	Summary of Events and Information.	Remarks and references to Appendices

1

WAR DIARY

or

INTELLIGENCE SUMMARY.

(Erase heading not required.)

Army Form C. 2118.

Instructions regarding War Diaries and Intelligence Summaries are contained in F. S. Regs., Part II, and the Staff Manual respectively. Title pages will be prepared in manuscript.

Hour, Date, Place.		Summary of Events and Information.	Remarks and references to Appendices
ST VAAST	14.12.14 (cont)	occupy position in square A4C (1/40,000 map) by 5 pm &	
	5 pm.	commence digging - all fairly dug in by 9.30 pm. First line with horses left at LE TOURET	
do	15.12.14	Misty day - make cover better & get out lines of fire - no action today	
do	16.12.14	Fire a few rounds to check lines - observ^n very difficult & would have to shoot at an area only -	
do	17.12.14	Withdrawn from trenches at about 2 pm the Bde being relieved	
	2 pm	by 13 Bde RFA - 8th Battery occupies a posn S.W. of ours to fire on our objective - Withdraw to LE TOURET for the	
LE TOURET	5 pm	night.	
PARADIS	18.12.14	March to billets at PARADIS about ½ mile NW of LOCON - start 8.30 am. Some rain & roads bad. occupy a flour mill & small paddock - sick horses	
	12 noon	separate in village - settle down by 12 noon -	
-	19.12.14	Aphtha disease being mastered, some of the cases being returned to duty - horses that had influenza very pulled down & debilitated -	
-	20.12.14 21.12.14	} Rest & exercise	

/

Army Form C. 2118.

WAR DIARY

or

INTELLIGENCE SUMMARY.

(Erase heading not required.)

Instructions regarding War Diaries and Intelligence Summaries are contained in F. S. Regs., Part II, and the Staff Manual respectively. Title pages will be prepared in manuscript.

Hour, Date, Place.	Summary of Events and Information.	Remarks and references to Appendices

A

War Diary
of
4th Brigade Ammunition Column R.F.A.

From 31-8-14
To 30-11-14

Volume I
Pp 1 to 5.

66 Battery R.H.A. 4 Bde R.F.A.
Meerut Div. Troops

Instructions regarding War Diaries and Intelligence Summaries are contained in F. S. Regs., Part II, and the Staff Manual respectively. Title pages will be prepared in manuscript.

WAR DIARY
or
INTELLIGENCE SUMMARY.

(Erase heading not required.)

Army Form C. 2118.

Hour, Date, Place.		Summary of Events and Information.	Remarks and references to Appendices.
1914			
October 26	6.30 am	Capt Theobald left Orleans with Corporal Reed 14th Battery & Corporal King 66th Battery on billeting duty for the Brigade by train. [illegible] joined the Battery from 19th Battery R.F.A.	
October 27	3.30 am	Above party arrived MERVILLE & selected billets for Brigade	
" 28		Battery left Orleans by train	
" 29		Battery arrived BERGUETTE 3.30 pm, marched to MERVILLE arrived 7.30 pm & billeted there for night.	
" 30		Marched at 3 pm arrived at les GLATIGNIES at 5 pm where Battery billeted.	
" 31		Battery left billets at 6 am & took up ~~an position~~ entrenched position about one mile West of RICHEBOURG L'AVOUE previously occupied by 119th Battery.	

Gulab Singh & Sons, Calcutta – No. 22 Army C. – 5 8 14 – 1,07,000

Instructions regarding War Diaries and Intelligence Summaries are contained in F. S. Regs., Part II, and the Staff Manual respectively. Title pages will be prepared in manuscript.

WAR DIARY
or
INTELLIGENCE SUMMARY.
(Erase heading not required.)

Army Form C. 2118.

5

Hour, Date, Place.	Summary of Events and Information	Remarks and references to Appendices.
October 31	Major Delaforce was in a Cottage and in communication by telephone with Observing Officer, Brigade Commander, Battery & Wagon Line. The observing Officer was Lieut Chance who was in front with the Infantry Commander. During the day only a few rounds were fired at the enemy's trenches to verify the Correction.	
November 1	Procedure same as previous day. Lieut Ellis was observing officer with the Infantry today.	
" 2	Battery relieved by 7th Battery at 7 a.m. Battery marched to position near LE TOURET, where it billetted in Farm Buildings. Gunners of Battery under Section Commanders & No 1's dug Gun Pits & trenches as a possible position	

Gulab Singh & Sons, Calcutta—No. 22 Army C.—5-8-14—1,07,000.

Army Form C. 2118.

6

Instructions regarding War Diaries and Intelligence Summaries are contained in F. S. Regs., Part II, and the Staff Manual respectively. Title pages will be prepared in manuscript.

WAR DIARY
or
INTELLIGENCE SUMMARY.

(*Erase heading not required.*)

Hour, Date, Place.	Summary of Events and Information	Remarks and references to Appendices.
November 2	in case of retirement in a field ½ mile SE of Scene S in Les FACONS facing Rue de BETHUNE	
3	Trenches completed by 12 noon today.	
	Horse AN2088 & BS/20146 died from rupture of intestine.	
4	Battery took over Guns & Equipment of 14th Battery RHA and relieved them from their position at E of CHAVATTES (on Map A Sheet). The Battery HQ were E of the Road & about 200x from the position. An officer from the Battery was in the Infantry Trenches day & night & in communication with the Battery HQ by telephone.	
5th } 6th }	Similar to above. Each day various German	

Gulab Singh & Sons, Calcutta—No. 22 Arms C.—5-8-14—1,07,000.

Instructions regarding War Diaries and Intelligence Summaries are contained in F. S. Regs., Part II, and the Staff Manual respectively. Title pages will be prepared in manuscript.

WAR DIARY

or

INTELLIGENCE SUMMARY.

(Erase heading not required.)

Army Form C. 2118.

7

Hour, Date, Place.	Summary of Events and Information	Remarks and references to Appendices.
Nov 5 & 6	Trenches & Batteries were shelled. The result appears to have been most effective	
7th	Battery relieved by 14th Battery & marched to billets in Le Touret. Horses guns etc in orchard men in sheds & barns.	
8	~~Left~~ Centre Section dug pits at a spot 200x E of Bde HQ nr Cse du RUILX with the object of bringing fire to bear on the German trenches in front of the Seaforth Highlanders. The lines were layed out by compass, the range about 5300x. The Section remained in position all night	
9	Left Section relieved Centre Section & improved gun pits	
10	Right Section relieved Left Section	

Gulab Singh & Sons, Calcutta—No. 22 Army C.—5-8-14—1,07,000.

or

INTELLIGENCE SUMMARY.

(*Erase heading not required.*)

Instructions regarding War Diaries and Intelligence Summaries are contained in F. S. Regs., Part II, and the Staff Manual respectively. Title pages will be prepared in manuscript.

8

Hour, Date, Place.	Summary of Events and Information	Remarks and references to Appendices.
November 11 – 15	One Section in Action, the remainder of Battery in billets at Le Touret. Usual procedure is for the Section to be relieved each morning at 7 a.m.	8
Nov 13/14	An attack was made on the German Trenches by the 20th Bde at 9 p.m. supported by Artillery Fire. During the night the Section in Action fired 120 rounds.	
14	Lieut Chance promoted Captain and took over command of the Bde Ammunition Column.	
15	Centre Section under fire from German Guns at 8 a.m. Gunner [illegible] wounded.	
16	Captain Holland joined Battery from 1st Bde Amn Column and posted as Right Section Commander	

Gulab Singh & Sons, Calcutta—No. 22 Army C.—5-8-14—1,07,000.

Instructions regarding War Diaries and Intelligence Summaries are contained in F. S. Regs., Part II, and the Staff Manual respectively. Title pages will be prepared in manuscript.

or

INTELLIGENCE SUMMARY.

(Erase heading not required.)

Hour, Date, Place.	Summary of Events and Information	Remarks and references to Appendices.
17 – 23 Nov	Battery in Reserve at Le Touret, with one Section in Action as before.	9
24 November	Battery relieved 7th Battery and occupied position about 800 SSE of RICHBOURG St VAAST Church, at 8 a.m. Battery is connected by Telephone with Bde HQ at Cse du Reulsc and with the Observing Officer in rear of our Infantry Trenches in a house in the Rue du Bois.	
25 – 28 "	In Action, desultory firing	
29 Nov	" Fired HE Shells on Enemy's Guns and trenches with apparent success.	

121/4146

War Diary of

4th Brigade R.F.A. Ammn Coln.

From 1-12-14
To 31-12-14

Volume I

Pp 6 to 8

Army Form C. 2118.

WAR DIARY
or
~~INTELLIGENCE SUMMARY.~~

(*Erase heading not required.*)

Instructions regarding War Diaries and Intelligence Summaries are contained in F. S. Regs., Part II, and the Staff Manual respectively. Title pages will be prepared in manuscript.

4th Brigade RFA
Ammunition Column

8

Hour, Date, Place.		Summary of Events and Information.	Remarks and references to Appendices.
LE CASAN	Dec 1st 1914	Weather was windy & mild.	Sadler admitted to hospital.
	Dec 2nd "	Nothing to report.	
	Dec 3rd "	"	
	Dec 4 "	"	
	Dec 5 "	"	
	Dec 6 "	"	One native driver to Hospital with pneumonia
	Dec 7 "	Very wet all day.	A/QMS Cloy joins for duty from 20th Battery RFA
	Dec 8 "	32 H.E. shell received from Divisional Amn. Coln.	
	Dec 9 "	Nothing to report	
	Dec 10 "	"	
	Dec 11	Captain A.F. Chance goes to England on leave.	
	Dec 12	"	
LA COUTURE	Dec 13	Moved Bivouac to enable 9th Bde AC to occupy LE CASSAN. Moved [illegible] at junction of Roads to LA COUTURE temporary until 34 SIKH PIONEERS VACATE	

Gulab Singh & Sons, Calcutta—No. 22 Army C.—5-8-14—1,07,000.

Army Form C. 2118.

WAR DIARY

or

INTELLIGENCE SUMMARY.

(Erase heading not required.)

Instructions regarding War Diaries and Intelligence Summaries are contained in F. S. Regs., Part II. and the Staff Manual respectively. Title pages will be prepared in manuscript.

Hour, Date, Place.	Summary of Events and Information.	Remarks and references to Appendices.
LA COUTURE	[illegible]	
ROBECQ	[illegible]	
Dec 18th	Captain A. F. Chance returned from [illegible] command [illegible] and [illegible]	
Dec 19th	[illegible]	

Gulab Singh & Sons, Calcutta—No. 22 Army C.—5-8-14—1,97,000.

Army Form C. 2118.

WAR DIARY
or
~~INTELLIGENCE SUMMARY.~~

(*Erase heading not* **required.**)

Instructions regarding War Diaries and Intelligence Summaries are contained in F. S. Regs., Part II, and the Staff Manual respectively. Title pages will be prepared in manuscript.

4th Brigade RFA
Ammunition Column.

6

Hour, Date, Place.		Summary of Events and Information.	Remarks and references to Appendices.
ROBECQ.	Dec 22nd	Nothing to report.	
	Dec 23rd	Lieut P.G.M. ELLES from 66th Battery joins for duty	
	Dec 24th	One horse cast and sent into Veterinary Section LOCON	
	Dec 25th.	Lieut Cockadey and 20 S.A.A. Carts Return from ESSARS.	
AMES	Dec 26th	Marched at 10 AM to AMES via LILLERS. Arrived AMES at 1°45 pm horses bivouaced in a field Men in farm houses; accomodation good.	afc..
	Dec 27th	Nothing to report.	
	Dec 28th	"	
	Dec 29th	"	
	Dec 30th	Completed ~~[illegible]~~ column with 18 PR ammunition from Divisional Column	
	Dec 31st		

Gulab Singh & Sons, Calcutta—No. 22 Army C.—5-8-14—1,07,000.

9th Divisional Ammunition Column

Renamed – 4th F.A. Brigade A.C.

Instructions regarding War Diaries and Intelligence Summaries are contained in F. S. Regs., Part II, and the Staff Manual respectively. Title pages will be prepared in manuscript.

WAR DIARY

or

INTELLIGENCE SUMMARY.

(Erase heading not required.)

Army Form C. 2118.

Hour, Date, Place.	Summary of Events and Information.	Remarks and references to Appendices
Trimulgherry 31.8.14	Received orders to mobilize [illegible]	[illegible]
TRIMULGHERRY 1.9.14	Mobilization Progress Normal C.H.	
2.	[illegible] C.H.	
3.	[illegible] C.H.	
4.	[illegible] C.H.	
5.	[illegible] C.H.	
6.	[illegible] C.H.	
7.	[illegible] C.H.	
8.	[illegible] C.H.	
9.	[illegible] C.H.	
10.	[illegible] C.H.	
11.	[illegible] C.H.	
12.	[illegible] C.H.	
13.	[illegible] C.H.	
14.	[illegible] C.H.	
15.	Mobilization complete. C.H.	
16.	[illegible]	[illegible]
17.	[illegible] C.H.	
18.	[illegible] C.H.	
19.	[illegible] C.H.	[illegible]
On Ships. 20.	[illegible] C.H.	
21.	[illegible] C.H.	
22.	[illegible] C.H.	
23.	[illegible] C.H.	
24.	[illegible] C.H.	
25.	[illegible] C.H.	
26.	[illegible] C.H.	
27.	[illegible] C.H.	

Gulab Singh & Sons, Calcutta—No. 22 Army C.—5-8-14—1,07,000.

9th Divisional Ammunition Column
Renamed:- 4th F.A. Bde A.C.

Instructions regarding War Diaries and Intelligence Summaries are contained in F. S. Regs., Part II, and the Staff Manual respectively. Title pages will be prepared in manuscript.

WAR DIARY
or
INTELLIGENCE SUMMARY.
(Erase heading not required.)

Army Form C. 2118

Sheet No 2.

Hour, Date, Place.		Summary of Events and Information.		Remarks and references to Appendices
On Ships	29.9.14	Convoy continues journey.	C.H.	(a). Left at Base 1 Native Gunner
	30. –	– do – . Onchorse dies on board S.S. Subadar.	C.H.	" " 1 " Driver, Sick.
	1. 10.14	– do – .	C.H.	" " 1 horse, lost.
	2. –	– do – .	C.H.	
	3. –	Both ships arrive ~~Suez~~ SUEZ & anchor off Canal mouth.	C.H.	at MARSEILLES.
	4. –	Remain at anchor	C.H.	
	5. –	Enter & pass through SUEZ CANAL	C.H.	
	6. –	Arrive PORT SAID at 4 a.m. Both ships anchor off Custom House.	C.H.	
	7. –	At 10 p.m. leave harbour. Convoy under French escort leaves at 4 p.m.	C.H.	
	8. –	Convoy continues journey.	C.H.	
	9. –	– do – .	C.H.	
	10. –	– do – .	C.H.	
	11. –	– do –	C.H.	
	12. –	– do – .	C.H.	
	13. –	– do – .		
	14. –	– do – .	C.H.	
MARSEILLES.	15. –	Arrive at MARSEILLES. Both ships commence dis embarkation in evening.	C.H.	
	16. –	Complete disembarkation. In evening camp in Parc BORELY, MARSEILLES. Weather very wet.	C.H.	
	17. –	Take over Indore Transport:- Officers Native 2, Indian Ranks 62, Followers 11, Ponies & mules 116, A.T. Carts 54.	C.H.	
	18. –	Entrain in two trains, as per ship (a) Indore Transport equally divided.	C.H.	
	19. –	Continue Train journey	C.H.	
ORLEANS.	20. –	Arrive ORLEANS, in evening & early morning 21st Oct. respectively.	C.H.	
	21. –	1st Train enters camp Les GROUES. 2nd Train arrives & enters camp. Weather dull.	C.H. C.H. C.H.	

Gulab Singh & Sons, Calcutta—No. 22 Army C.—5-8-14—1,07,000.

4 F.A. Brigade A.C.

Sheet No 3

Army Form C. 2118.

Instructions regarding War Diaries and Intelligence Summaries are contained in F. S. Regs., Part II, and the Staff Manual respectively. Title pages will be prepared in manuscript.

WAR DIARY
or
INTELLIGENCE SUMMARY.

(*Erase heading not required.*)

Hour, Date, Place.	Summary of Events and Information.	Remarks and references to Appendices
ORLEANS 22-10-14.	Remain in camp. Drew stores to complete. [illegible]	[illegible]
23-10-14.	[illegible]	[illegible]
	[illegible]	
24		
25		
26		
27		
28	Entrained at Les Aubrais station in two trains. 1st train left at 7.30 a.m.	
29	Arrived [illegible] at 7 p.m. Marched to Merville.	
30	2nd Train [illegible] Merville at 10 a.m. Marched to bivouac at ~~[illegible]~~ MERVILLE	
MERVILLE ~~LES FACONS~~ 31	Marched from MERVILLE to LES FACONS (bivouac) [illegible]	
LES FACONS 1st Nov. 14.	Remained in bivouac at LES FACONS & supplied the 4th Bde RFA with ammunition also 20th Inf Bde.	
2		
3		
4		
5		

Gulab Singh & Sons, Calcutta—No. 22 Army C.—5-8-14—1,07,000.

4th F.A. Brigade A.C.

Army Form C. 2118.

Sheet 4

WAR DIARY

or

~~INTELLIGENCE SUMMARY.~~

(Erase heading not required.)

Instructions regarding War Diaries and Intelligence Summaries are contained in F. S. Regs., Part II, and the Staff Manual respectively. Title pages will be prepared in manuscript.

Hour, Date, Place.	Summary of Events and Information.	Remarks and references to Appendices.
LES FACONS 8th Nov. 1914	Remained in bivouac	
LECASAN 9th	Marched to LE CASAN & bivouacked there. Horses picketed in the open. Men in barns.	
10th		
11th	do	
12th	"	
13th	"	
14th	Capt CROFTON left on posting to 7th Battery RFA.	A[illegible]
15th	Capt CHANCE from 66th Battery RFA assumes command.	
	One horse sick with 'PINK EYE' & immediately isolated.	
16th	Capt HOLLAND left on posting to 66th Battery RFA.	
17th	—	
18th	—	3 horses sent to Field. Vety Secn
19th	Snow fell from midday till after dark and there was frost at night	
20th	Roads very slippery for horses	

Gulab Singh & Sons, Calcutta—No. 22 Army C.—5-8-14—1,07,000.

Army Form C. 2118.

WAR DIARY

or

INTELLIGENCE SUMMARY.

(Erase heading not required.)

Instructions regarding War Diaries and Intelligence Summaries are contained in F. S. Regs., Part II, and the Staff Manual respectively. Title pages will be prepared in manuscript.

Hour, Date, Place.	Summary of Events and Information.	Remarks and references to Appendices.
LE CASAN 21 Nov. 1914		
22 Nov	Very hard frost	
23 Nov	ditto	
24 Nov	A thaw set in	
25		
26		
27	Rain & stormy weather	
28	Changed horse lines to another field on account of wet state of ground	
29		
30		

Gulab Singh & Sons, Calcutta—No. 22 Army C.—5-8-14—1,07,000.

A

121/4401

WAR DIARY

OF

56th Battery R.F.A.

From 1st January 1915 To, 31st January 1915

27.1.15 was with 32nd Bde R.F.A. 8th Division

101

Instructions regarding War Diaries and Intelligence Summaries are contained in F. S. Regs., Part II. and the Staff Manual respectively. Title pages will be prepared in manuscript.

WAR DIARY
or
~~INTELLIGENCE~~ SUMMARY.
(Erase heading not required.)

Army Form C. 2118.

Hour, Date, Place	Summary of Events and Information	Remarks and references to Appendices

(9 29 6) W4141—463 100,000 9/14 H W V Forms/C. 2118/10

Instructions regarding War Diaries and Intelligence Summaries are contained in F. S. Regs., Part II. and the Staff Manual respectively. Title pages will be prepared in manuscript.

WAR DIARY
or
~~INTELLIGENCE SUMMARY.~~
(Erase heading not required.)

Army Form C. 2118.

56th Bty R.F.A.

Hour, Date, Place	Summary of Events and Information	Remarks and references to Appendices
17 · 1 · 15 LESPESSES		
18 · 1 · 15 "		
19 · 1 · 15 "		
20 · 1 · 15 "		
21 · 1 · 15 "	Routine work in billets.	
22 · 1 · 15 "		
23 · 1 · 15 "		
24 · 1 · 15 "		
25 · 1 · 15 "		
26 · 1 · 15 CALONNE	Received orders at 1.50 pm to proceed to CALONNE en route to join 4th Corps. C.O to LA GORGUE for orders from 8th Divn. Battery marched at 4 pm. via LILLERS and ROBECQ and billeted in CALONNE at 8 p.m.	
27 · 1 · 15. CROIX-BARBÉE	Battery marched at 1.30 pm and occupied a position 400 yds S. of CROIX-BARBÉE in support of 24th Inf. Bde, being attached by G.O.C.R.A. 8th Divn to 33rd Bde R.F.A. Wagon line at PETIT-MARAIS.	
28 · 1 · 15 CROIX BARBÉE	Observing from house 300 yds W.S.W. of junction of RUE DU BOIS and main ESTAIRE-LA BASSÉE road, registered German trenches E and SE of cross roads.	M.

(9 29 6) W4141—463 100,000 9/14 H W V Forms/C. 2118/10

Instructions regarding War Diaries and Intelligence Summaries are contained in F. S. Regs., Part II. and the Staff Manual respectively. Title pages will be prepared in manuscript.

WAR DIARY

or

~~INTELLIGENCE~~ SUMMARY.

(Erase heading not required.)

Army Form C. 2118.

Hour, Date, Place	Summary of Events and Information	Remarks and references to Appendices

121/4401

WAR DIARY

OF

4th Brigade, R. F. A.

From 1-1-15 To 31-1-15.

Instructions regarding War Diaries and Intelligence Summaries are contained in F. S. Regs., Part II, and the Staff Manual respectively. Title pages will be prepared in manuscript.

WAR DIARY

or

INTELLIGENCE SUMMARY.

(Erase heading not required.)

Army Form C. 2118.

Hour, Date, Place.	Summary of Events and Information.	Remarks and references to Appendices
1 - January 1915	The 14th Brigade R.H.A. remained in billets at AIRES and Bellery.	Lieut Mason replaced Lieut Ellis in 66th Battery on 23rd Dec & the latter went to 4th Bde AC RHA
6 - 1 - 15 12.15 PM	The Brigade was inspected (dismounted) by the Indian Corps Commander.	
7 - 1 - 15	Lieut Colonels A.D. KIRBY & W.J.K. RETTIE left the Brigade for England. Captain Holland went to 13th Brigade AC from 66th Battery, Capt Colfox left 14th Battery to join 5th Divn. Lieut Fraser & Dodds joined 14th & 66th Batteries respectively.	
8 - 1 - 15	2Lieut Parcell joined 14th Battery & Capt Rutherford left 14th Battery to command 4th Brigade AC RHA. Major Taylor joined to command 14th Battery RHA.	[illegible] Lieut Colonel [illegible] Gordon left for [illegible]
11 - 1 - 15	Major Parrington joined to command 7th Battery RHA. The officers in 14th Bde are now as under. Lieut Colonel L.W.G. Gordon RHA Comdg, Capt R.B. Ward (?) Adjutant. 7th Bty. Major ~~Taylor~~ J.R. PARRINGTON, Capt M.A.A. CROFTON, Lieut R.D. [illegible], LT BABBAGE, 2LT. G RIDDLE. 14th Battery. Major B.W. Taylor, Capt P Turnbull, LT W.D. Pritchard, 2Lieut D.F. FRASER, 2Lieut C.B.T. PARCELL	Herbert [illegible] in [illegible] of CRA

Gulab Singh & Sons, Calcutta—No. 22 Army C.—5-8-14—1,07,000.

Army Form C. 2118.

WAR DIARY

or

INTELLIGENCE SUMMARY.

(Erase heading not required.)

Instructions regarding War Diaries and Intelligence Summaries are contained in F. S. Regs., Part II, and the Staff Manual respectively. Title pages will be prepared in manuscript.

Hour, Date, Place.	Summary of Events and Information.	Remarks and references to Appendices
	66th Battery R.F.A. Major E L DELAFORCE, Capt. A.L.L. THEOBALD, 2LT G.N.C MARTIN, 2LT A.A. MARSON, 2LT. T.E DODDS.	
	4th Bde Ammunition Column R.F.A. CAPT. RUTHERFOORD. LT P.G.M. ELLIS, LT. (QM) W.G.C. COCKADAY.	
	Attached Capt. A.E.B JONES. RAMC. + LT. D.A.S. BECK A.V.C	
18-1-15	Lieut W.D. PRITCHARD was selected to undergo a course of aerial observation & was temporarily attached to No 35 Coy. Flying Corps.	
15-1-15	LIEUT PRITCHARD returned	
21-1-15	MAJOR J.W.P. PAYNTER joined to command 14th Battery in place of MAJOR TAYLOR posted to to 13th Bde R.F.A.	
31-1-15	2LIEUT. MARTIN left 4th Bde on appointment to R.H.A. LIEUT. P.G.M ELLIS transferred from 4th Bde A.C. R.F.A. to 66th Battery R.F.A.	
	R B Warton Capt RFA for O.C. 4th Bde R.F.A.	

Gulab Singh & Sons, Calcutta—No. 22 Army C.—5-8-14—1,07,000.

Feb 1915

4th Bde R.F.A.

On His Majesty's Service.

Confidential

War Diaries
Western Frontier
Force

The Secretary

War Office

London

S. W.

28
II BRIGADE R.F.A.
1 — 28 Feb 1915

Serial No. 38

121/4719

WAR DIARY

4th Brigade R.F.A.

From 1st February 1915 To 28th February 1915

Army Form C. 2118.

Instructions regarding War Diaries and Intelligence Summaries are contained in F. S. Regs., Part II, and the Staff Manual respectively. Title pages will be prepared in manuscript.

WAR DIARY

or

INTELLIGENCE SUMMARY.

(Erase heading not required.)

Hour, Date, Place.	Summary of Events and Information.	Remarks and references to Appendices
1-2-15	The H.Qrs Staff at AMES but 7th 14th 66 Batteries & 4th Bde AC [illegible]	
	Orders received for B.C.s & observing officers with detachments to	
	go up to LACOUTURE so as to take over from 18th 40th & 7th Batteries	
3-2-15 2 PM	7th & 14th Batteries moved into action at LA CROIX MARMUSE, 66 Battery	
	in reserve at CROIX MARMUSE. 4th Bde AC to LES LOBES. The	
	Brigade marched via VILLERS, CHOCQUES, HINGES & LOCON.	
	Batteries verified night lines & registered points in hostile lines.	
4 PM	14th Battery fired 2 shell at machine gun in S10 hitting the	
9.45	parapet. Range & line taken from map. Some German shell fell	
	near 14th Battery billets at 8 PM.	
4-2-15	7th & 14th Batteries registered lines of fire.	
2.30 PM	7th Battery fired rounds at machine gun emplacements in	
	enemy trenches afterwards lines were registered.	
10.15 AM	14th Battery fired at German working party near [illegible]	
[illegible]	shelled small party of Germans seen near [illegible]	
	[illegible] 4 out of 6 shell struck the house.	
1.35	Germans seen repairing machine gun emplacement [illegible]	
4.30 pm	14th fired on group of enemy & at 5.10 pm on machine gun	
5.10 pm	14th shelled German trenches whilst our infantry relief were taking place.	
	Night quiet.	
5-2-15	7th Battery continued registering & moved their guns into our position instead	
	of having sections separated.	

Gulab Singh & Sons, Calcutta—No. 22 Army C.—5-8-14—1,07,000.

Army Form C. 2118.

Instructions regarding War Diaries and Intelligence Summaries are contained in F. S. Regs., Part II, and the Staff Manual respectively. Title pages will be prepared in manuscript.

WAR DIARY
or
INTELLIGENCE SUMMARY.

(Erase heading not required.)

Hour, Date, Place.	Summary of Events and Information.	Remarks and references to Appendices
5-2-1915 12.40 pm	14th Battery opened on a German barricade on road near BOIS DE BIEZ. A German battery was located near BOIS DE BIEZ but it was too dark to observe. German batteries active & houses	
3.35 pm	500 yds from 14th Battery set on fire. 7th Bty registered various lines	
6-2-1915	At 7.30 the 14th Battery shelled 30 Germans crossing barricade in S5c at at 12 noon drove the enemy out of a house S11b where they had been seen collecting. A machine gun post in S10b and the enemy's support trenches were shelled in the afternoon this was in cooperation with 2nd Divn attack. The enemy artillery was active during the day & at 2pm the 7th Bty observation post was shelled after 7th Bty had registered some communication	Ref map Sheet 36. 1 in 40000 France 13 Series
4 pm	trenches. At 4pm the 14th Bty silenced the enemy's sharpshooters and at 6 & 9pm delivered sudden burst of fire on some machine gun emplacement in S5c with great effect. The Infy reported that they heard screams from the German trenches	
7-2-1915 8am	At 8am the 14th Bty shelled a barricade in S15b and at 10am 7th Battery stopped enemy's shell fire by shelling the distillery No 51. which was probably the German observation post. At 2.15 the 7th Bty also shelled communication trench between 8c 155 where activity had been observed the result appeared good	

Gulab Singh & Sons, Calcutta—No. 22 Army C.—5-8-14—1,07,000.

Army Form C. 2118.

Instructions regarding War Diaries and Intelligence Summaries are contained in F. S. Regs., Part II, and the Staff Manual respectively. Title pages will be prepared in manuscript.

WAR DIARY
or
INTELLIGENCE SUMMARY.
(Erase heading not required.)

Hour, Date, Place.	Summary of Events and Information.	Remarks and references to Appendices
7-2-1915	At 4 PM the 7th Observation Post was again shelled & the 7th in conjunction with the 110th heavy battery shelled enemy's battery No 52 & silenced hostile fire. At 4.45 a party of Germans leaving the barricade were shelled in S106 with good effect by 1st Bty. Young officers were sent up to the Observation Stations for instruction	No 52 S.E. near LA BASSEE Road, [illegible]
9.15 PM	The 1st silenced hostile machine gun with 2 rounds & the infantry were not troubled by it again. The Army [illegible] gun fire & 3 German shells fell near the 1st Bty position	
8-2-1915	Nothing of importance occurred till 10 AM when 7th Battery again silenced enemy's fire on the observation post by shelling hostile battery near LORGIES [illegible] from 10.46 to 1.22 the 1st Battery fired at intervals on barricades S.W. of BOIS DE BIEZ & near RICHEBOURG L'AVOUE with some considerable effect. At 11.20 the 7th Battery shelled enemy's trenches in front of RICHEBOURG L'AVOUE & silenced musketry fire and at 2 PM shelled the barricade on LA BASSEE Road. The infantry reported the fire of both batteries as very good.	

Gulab Singh & Sons, Calcutta—No. 22 Army C.—5-8-11—1,07,000.

Army Form C. 2118.

Instructions regarding War Diaries and Intelligence Summaries are contained in F. S. Regs., Part II, and the Staff Manual respectively. Title pages will be prepared in manuscript.

WAR DIARY

or

INTELLIGENCE SUMMARY.

(*Erase heading not required.*)

Hour, Date, Place.	Summary of Events and Information.	Remarks and references to Appendices
	The night 8–9th February was very quiet	
9-2-15.	At 7.45 am & 8.30 am the 14th Battery fired a few rounds at the	
7.45 Am	enemy's trenches where the smoke of fires was visible & at 7.50 am	
to	they hit the parapet where a hostile machine gun had been located	
	Occasional shots were fired at the barricade on LA BASSEE	
8.45 Am	ROAD S5a till 8.45 am.	
10-10 Am	At 10.10 am a hostile battery opened fire from direction of	
	BOIS DE BIEZ the shell falling 200 yards short of 14th Bty.	
	Information was immediately sent to 8th Divn (33rd FA Bde)	
9 am	who cooperated & the hostile fire was stopped. At 9 am	
	The 7th Bty O.P. had been shelled by a German field battery	
	from direction of the distillery which was stopped as before	
	by shelling the hostile battery at LORGIES. A few rounds	
	were fired to register houses & points in the German line	
1.20	till 1.20 when both 7th & 14th Batteries turned their fire onto	
	a prominent red house reported by the infantry to contain	
	a gun. Four direct hits & 5 shell in outbuildings behind	
	was the result which threw up a lot of dust. Later a	Lieut Colonel BLUNT MACKENZIE
4.30	few rounds were fired by both batteries at Germans seen	Major ~~Crocker~~ CROOKER
	at Barricade S5c. The officers mentioned in margin joined	Capt Hatfield
	from the Army at Home for instruction	Lt Deedes.

Gulab Singh & Sons, Calcutta—No. 22 Army C.—5-8-14—1,07,000.

Army Form C. 2118.

WAR DIARY
or
INTELLIGENCE SUMMARY.
(*Erase heading not required.*)

Instructions regarding War Diaries and Intelligence Summaries are contained in F. S. Regs., Part II, and the Staff Manual respectively. Title pages will be prepared in manuscript.

Hour, Date, Place.	Summary of Events and Information.	Remarks and references to Appendices
9 – 2 – 15 9.15pm & 10pm.	A series of Shell burst round 14th Bty Head Quarters the Majority being to the north.	
10 · 2 · 15. 7.15am	During the morning the 1st Battery shelled enemy crossing the barricade on SET La Bassee Road three times & some casualties were noted. Enemy's trenches were also shelled & this was [illegible] repeated. During the afternoon activity was again seen at the barricade when the Germans were seen with wheelbarrows & carrying planks. Our fire was effective.	
11.20	At 11.20 the 7th Battery also reported great activity in a trench leading to a redoubt opposite the RUE DE BOIS the 7th Bty opened an effective fire and at 11.45 am shelled Barricade on La Bassee Road in conjunction with the 2nd Siege Battery. At 12.45 fire was turned again on the above mentioned redoubt where activity was again noted. At 3pm the 7th Bty in conjunction with the 2nd Heavy Siege battery again shelled the redoubt where activity had begun again & effectually stopped their work	
3.45 – 4.15	Hostile battery unlocated shelled RUE DE BOIS.	

Gulab Singh & Sons. Calcutta—No. 22 Army C.—5-8-14—1,07,000.

Army Form C. 2118.

Instructions regarding War Diaries and Intelligence Summaries are contained in F. S. Regs., Part II, and the Staff Manual respectively. Title pages will be prepared in manuscript.

WAR DIARY
or
INTELLIGENCE SUMMARY.

(Erase heading not required.)

Hour, Date, Place.	Summary of Events and Information.	Remarks and references to Appendices
10 pm 9-2-15	Green signal rockets seen in direction of NEUVE CHAPELLE	
11 PM	Six German shell burst about 400 yds E of Bty position (16th Bty)	
11-2-15	There was thick mist in the morning and very little shooting possible. At 10.10 the 12th Battery & 2nd Siege in cooperation shelled	
10.10a	trench & redoubt in S10b. but no enemy seen.	
1.55 pm	The 8th Divn reported a battery firing on their trenches & 12th Battery shelled on S11a, one shell striking house & the remainder falling just behind in orchard where enemy's battery supposed to be. The 7th Battery put a fine shell on barricade S10b & on enemy's trenches. In the afternoon alternative guns positions were dug & prepared & a few more points registered.	
5.22	The 8th Divn signal S.O.S was sent through on telephone & battery reported they had fired in 4 minutes. The 7th Battery O.P. was shelled in the morning & Observation Officer obliged to withdraw temporarily	This signal S.O.S is sent when a hostile attack suddenly takes place, each battery opens fire on a prearranged target in aid of 8th Divn.
12-2-15	A quiet night. During the morning of 12th both batteries fired at small parties of Germans seen at the two road barricades & communication trenches	
2 pm	At 2pm the 12th Battery cooperated with a field Howitzer battery in shelling enemy's trenches & redoubt in S10d. (SE of RICHEBOURG L'AVOUE) At 2.45 a house was shelled in S11a SW of BOIS DE BIEZ 2 H.E. shell struck the wall. Enemy very quiet in the afternoon.	

Gulab Singh & Sons, Calcutta—No. 22 Army C.—5-8-14—1,07,000.

Army Form C. 2118.

Instructions regarding War Diaries and Intelligence Summaries are contained in F. S. Regs., Part II, and the Staff Manual respectively. Title pages will be prepared in manuscript.

WAR DIARY
or
INTELLIGENCE SUMMARY.

(Erase heading not required.)

Hour, Date, Place.	Summary of Events and Information.	Remarks and references to Appendices
12-2-1915 9.30am	The Enemy shelled houses & factory near 7th Battery O.P. At 12 noon the 7th Battery fired on redoubt in S10d in conjunction with 2nd Siege battery & drove the enemy out. This was repeated at 12.30, 1.15 PM as enemy returned. The fire was however very effective & the enemy left again. At 1.42 a hostile battery opened fire on houses near 7th Bty O.P.	
2 PM.	The 7th Bty again shelled redoubt in cooperation with Siege battery with great effect. The enemy again retired & hostile	A blind shell found near Observation Post, was painted yellow, base diameter 75mm marked on edge [illegible] Dopp K.Z. 96.
3PM, 4PM	battery shelled the 7th Bty O.P. at 3PM and at 4PM. The hostile battery was not located but fire came from direction of LORGIES.	
13-2-1915 7-8 AM	Many Germans seen carrying planks, hurdles & [illegible] in their trenches & especially in communication trench near barricade near BOIS DE BIEZ. 14th Battery fired 10 rounds of which appeared very effective though only two were [illegible] burst.	
10 AM	At 10 am the 7th Battery opened fire on cross roads where a brushwood screen was visible concealing enemy's movements on LA BASSEE Road. The 14th Bty observing officer reported that at 10 am two very effective rounds fell on parapet of German fire trench.	
9.30 AM	At 9.30 am a German battery	

Gulab Singh & Sons, Calcutta—No. 22 Army C.—5-8-14—1,07,000.

Army Form C. 2118.

WAR DIARY
or
INTELLIGENCE SUMMARY.

(Erase heading not required.)

Instructions regarding War Diaries and Intelligence Summaries are contained in F. S. Regs., Part II, and the Staff Manual respectively. Title pages will be prepared in manuscript.

Hour, Date, Place.	Summary of Events and Information.	Remarks and references to Appendices
13 - 2 - 15	fired 6 rounds in direction of 14th Battery. The batteries were relieved by 11th Brigade R.F.A. by noon & the 4th Brigade went back to LA BRASSERIE near ROBECQ into billets.	
13th to 25th	Remained in billets at LA BRASSERIE. 2nd Lieut OLIVER JONES and 2nd Lt CAMPBELL GRANT joined with temporary Commissions. Reconnaissance work was carried out & artillery positions in secondary lines chosen	
25th - 2 - 15	4th Brigade marched to positions. 7th Bty in reserve at LA CROIX MARMUSE, 14th & 66th Batteries to action at LA CROIX BARBEE AtBde AC to ZELOBES & HQ 4 Bde to LA COUTURE. The 74th & 66th Batteries took over positions from 85th & 86th Btys respectively. The afternoon was occupied in registering and verifying lines of fire	
10.25 PM	No 3 Infantry picquet was forced to take cover in trenches full of water from hostile machine gun & rifle fire. 66th Battery fired 5 rounds No 3 picket reporting that Shell burst in enemy's trenches causing great commotion. No further trouble was experienced by our infantry.	
26 - 2 - 15.	The morning was misty an no firing occurred till 11am when registration was continued by 66th Battery who had trouble with Mark V ×Shell which fell very short. Mark II shell used at 3PM were quite satisfactory. at 3.15 the 66th fired 20 shell with good effect on hostile trenches. This was to baffle new German formations reported by infantry	× probably due to fuzes

Instructions regarding War Diaries and Intelligence Summaries are contained in F. S. Regs., Part II, and the Staff Manual respectively. Title pages will be prepared in manuscript.

WAR DIARY

or

INTELLIGENCE SUMMARY.

(Erase heading not required.)

Army Form C. 2118.

Hour, Date, Place.	Summary of Events and Information.	Remarks and references to Appendices
26-2-1915 11.30	The 14th Battery fired a few rounds at enemy seen walking about in fire trenches & at noon registered a barricade on LA BASSEE road & got good burst on some snipers.	Infantry line at Richebourg ST VAAST
1 PM	Hostile battery opened fire from direction of BOIS du BIEZ	No 3 Subsection } 1st Seaforths
2.55	Ten rounds were fired on German trenches to retaliate new German formation. Effective. At 3.30 the enemy's infantry again seen walking in fire trenches - 11 rounds majority effective made them take cover.	No 2 Subsection } 2 Gurkhas
8.15 PM	66th Battery shelled hostile machine gun in front of C Section & at 9.5 PM shelled machine gun on cinder track.	No one Subsection } 1st Seaforths
27.2.15.	Lieut R.B. Batts joined with Temporary Commission & posted to 4th Bde. Am. Col. — Captain & Adjutant R.B. Warton wounded in leg by a Shrapnel Bullet — and removed to Hospital at MERVILLE — Captain P. TURNBULL 14th Battery taking his place as Acting Adjutant —	
11.55 am	14th Battery fired a few Rds at Snipers in Enemy's fire Trench. 66th Battery fired 10 Rds MK I Shell for testing purposes — fuzes irregular —	
2.55 pm.	66th had a few Rds on Enemy's machine gun — Effect appeared most effective —	
28-2-15.	Another quiet night — Capt Warton sent back to BOULOGNE	

Gulab Singh & Sons, Calcutta—No. 22 Army C.—5-8-14—1,07,000.

Army Form C. 2118.

WAR DIARY

or

INTELLIGENCE SUMMARY.

(Erase heading not required.)

Instructions regarding War Diaries and Intelligence Summaries are contained in F. S. Regs., Part II, and the Staff Manual respectively. Title pages will be prepared in manuscript.

Hour, Date, Place.		Summary of Events and Information.	Remarks and references to Appendices
28.2.15	7.45am	14th Battery fired a few rounds at German working party behind fire trench — They fired at probable observing station at a house where they saw a few men enter —	
	11.45am } 12.1pm }	a few Rounds fired at snipers in German trench — ~~Corr~~ Corrector for day 142 with uncapped fuzes —	
	3.30pm	Three small shell burst in field close to 14th Battery, fuzes set at 44½ — Several periscopes were seen during the day ~~in~~ redoubt in front of No 2 Section —	
	4.45pm	Part of redoubt was seen to be on fire — 66th fired a few Rounds into it — Another quiet evening —	

[signature] Turnbull Capt.
Adj IV Bde RFA.

5/3/15

Gulab Singh & Sons, Calcutta—No. 22 Army C.—5-8-14—1,07,000.

Meerut

IV. Brigade R.F.A.

1st March 1915 31st March 1915

Instructions regarding War Diaries and Intelligence Summaries are contained in F. S. Regs., Part II, and the Staff Manual respectively. Title pages will be prepared in manuscript.

Army Form C. 2118.

WAR DIARY
or
INTELLIGENCE SUMMARY.
(Erase heading not required.)

IV Bde RFA.
March 1914

Hour, Date, Place.	Summary of Events and Information.	Remarks and references to Appendices
1. 3. 15 — 7am	14th Bty. fired at reliefs entering fire trench without rifles —	MAP. FRANCE Sheet 36 SW 1/20,000
12.1pm	Shelled Machine Gun parapet as pointed out by our Infantry — one Round hit top of parapet —	
3pm	Fired a few Rounds at men carrying sacks in Communicating trench — Three men were seen in enemy's Support trench dressed in Khaki similar to our own with brown balaclava hats —	
1 – 4pm	Prepared platforms for new position + laid out lines —	
10 am	66th Bty — fired a few Rds on enemy's guns located by flashes — Iron plates thought to be machine gun shields were fired on — 2 plates were in fire trench + 2 in Support trench —	
2pm	A few Rds were fired into Redoubt where movement was seen —	
	7th Battery still in Reserve	
7.15pm	14th Bty fired two effective Rds at machine guns which were annoying our Infantry	
2. 3. 15 —	7th Battery went into action about a mile S.E. of LA COUTURE and Registered day + night lines —	
7am	14th Bty fired at enemy's reliefs coming into trenches —	
8am	Right Section moved into new position ~~[illegible]~~ and started Registration —	
10am	Remainder of Battery came into new position —	
3pm	a few Rounds were fired on Party of Germans walking in Communication trench	
3.30pm	Fired on Snipers in picquet post —	
4.50pm	Registered probable observing post as our Infantry reported it occupied by the enemy —	
6.30pm	Three Rds were fired at Machine Guns while our Infantry were being relieved —	
	66th Bty —	
11am	German Redoubt shelled with aeroplane observing with satisfactory Result — The first time any of the Batteries fired with the assistance of an aeroplane — 12 Rds were fired of which 4 were reported as Target + the others very close —	

Gulab Singh & Sons, Calcutta—No. 22 Army C.—5-8-14—1,07,000.

Instructions regarding War Diaries and Intelligence Summaries are contained in F. S. Regs., Part II, and the Staff Manual respectively. Title pages will be prepared in manuscript.

WAR DIARY
or
INTELLIGENCE SUMMARY.
(Erase heading not required.)

Army Form C. 2118.

Hour, Date, Place.	Summary of Events and Information.	Remarks and references to Appendices
2. 3. 15.	There was much movement in the afternoon in the German trenches & a few men were seen to be wearing caps with red head bands	
4.30 pm	A likely observing house was shelled & 10 direct hits obtained —	
	The DEHRA DUN Bde were relieved by BAREILLY Bde — about 7. pm — Infantry line divided into four Subsections as per margin —	A 41st Dogras — B 9th Gurkhas — 66th Bty C Royal Highlanders 14th " D 6th Jats — 7th "
3. 3. 15 —	A quiet night nothing to Report —	
	7th Bty. A German Battery shelled RICHEBOURG ST VAAST. Battery could not be located — observing officer selected a new observing Post in the trenches at the extreme left of "D" Subsection —	
7.35 am	14th Bty. Smoke and men seen issuing from house in S5a on which one direct hit was obtained.	
8.35 am	Parties of enemy passing down communication trench in S5c were fired on —	
9.35 am	Registered Bridge across ditch in German fire trench —	
10.55 "	Fired on houses & Road in S5b where party of Germans were seen —	
11.40 "	Fired on house on LA BASSEE — ESTAIRES Road in S10b, reported by Royal Highlanders in "PORT ARTHUR" as German observation post —	
1.35 pm	fired at Snipers in S10b with good effect —	
3 — 3.30 pm	German Battery shelled observation station — Fired at Battery in S17b.	
5. pm	Fired at party of Germans carrying planks in communication trench —	
6 pm	Connected up by telephone with PORT ARTHUR —	
8. pm	Signal light seen in direction of AUBERS from PORT ARTHUR —	
	66th Bty. Ready to fire at 7am. with assistance of aeroplane but owing to bad weather it did not turn up —	
3.30 pm & 4.40 pm	Fired at redoubt in co-operation with 2nd Siege Bty RGA.	
8.45 pm	fired 6 Rounds on enemy's trenches to stop their rifle fire —	

Gulab Singh & Sons, Calcutta—No. 22 Army C.—5 8 14—1,07,000.

Army Form C. 2118.

Instructions regarding War Diaries and Intelligence Summaries are contained in F. S. Regs., Part II, and the Staff Manual respectively. Title pages will be prepared in manuscript.

WAR DIARY
or
INTELLIGENCE SUMMARY.
(*Erase heading not required.*)

Hour, Date, Place.		Summary of Events and Information.	Remarks and references to Appendices
		7th Bty –	
4.3.15.	9 a.m.	Six Rounds were fired on North half of D Subsection on German trenches where enemy were observed to be active –	MAP FRANCE Sheet 36 S.W.
	12.40 pm	fired a few Rounds (effective) on German Machine Gun in Trench S4657 An advanced O.P. has been opened in the trenches (known by Infantry as THE LINK	
		14th Bty	
	8.45 am	Fired 5 Rounds at party carrying Sandbags in Communicating trench & Redoubt S10662	
	10. am	Fired a few Rounds at snipers firing at our Aeroplane – new dark grey uniform seen here with peaked cap. black peak –	
	11.15 a.m.	Experimented with lashed wheels & fixed trail – wheels on half filled sandbags – Gun sunk for five Rds & then remained stationary –	
	1.30 pm	Fired on parties entering fire trench from Redoubt S10b –	
	3.20 pm	PORT ARTHUR was shelled by enemy – one Section replied & fired four Rounds into fire trench opposite – Another Section fire on guns at 86 in S17a and 2 Rounds at Distillery – German Shelling ceased –	
	7. pm	Fired one Round on Machine Gun in S10c 5.5. at request of Infantry –	
		66th Bty	
	7.20 am	Fired a few Rounds at Redoubt which the Germans were repairing –	
	9.15 am	Ranged with assistance of aeroplane on emplacements in S6a99 – Range not found & no other Target could be taken on owing to the Mist –	
5.3.15.	12 noon	Registered enemy's trenches –	
	2.15 pm	a German Bty (PIPSQUEAK) shelled our Salient S4622 & the Bty Replied by shelling the German trenches – fire appeared v. effective	
	3.30 pm	a German Bty from the direction of NEUVE CHAPELLE shelled RICHEBOURG ST VAAST	

Army Form C. 2118.

WAR DIARY
or
INTELLIGENCE SUMMARY.
(Erase heading not required.)

Instructions regarding War Diaries and Intelligence Summaries are contained in F. S. Regs., Part II, and the Staff Manual respectively. Title pages will be prepared in manuscript.

Hour, Date, Place.	Summary of Events and Information.	Remarks and references to Appendices
5.3.15	14th Bty. Registered German trenches. One officer in observing Post + one in PORT ARTHUR. Latter place shelled from Distillery S.17a.	
2.30 pm	Shelled ruined house in S17a 36 as Infantry reported enemy's observer there. (This house likely O.P. for German Howitzer Battery)	
6 pm	Several effective Rounds fired on a party of about 60 Germans leaving fire trench via Redoubt S10b.	
7 am	66th Bty. fired 4 Rds at enemy working pump in their trenches.	
12.30 pm	opened fire on house at S10d 96. This house seemed to be observing station for 'PIPSQUEAK' Bty.	
1.10 pm + 5 pm	fired on working party in Redoubt S10d.	
8 pm	fired a few Rds on enemy's Machine Gun + made it stop firing.	
6.3.15.	7th Bty.	
4.30 am to 7 am	Very heavy firing was heard somewhere North + on our left.	
11 am + 11.30 am	Two German Batteries opened fire on our trenches.	
3 pm	Registered a few points on German trenches.	
	16th Bty.	
8.9 am	Two Rounds fired to verify yesterday's Registration. Very Satisfactory.	
11 am to 11.30 am	Enemy's field Howitzer threw shell near O.P. – fired 10 Rounds into enemy's probable O.P. in S17a + Distillery behind. One burst in window of O.P.	
2.20 pm	Registered trench in S5c 453, also fork S11a 78.	
3.25 to 3.65 pm	fairly heavy fire heard in direction of FESUIBERT	
3.50 pm	Vicinity of O.P. shelled from direction of Distillery. 3 Rds struck house in rear.	

Gulab Singh & Sons, Calcutta—No. 22 Army C.—5-8-14—1,07,000.

Army Form C. 2118.

Instructions regarding War Diaries and Intelligence Summaries are contained in F. S. Regs., Part II, and the Staff Manual respectively. Title pages will be prepared in manuscript.

WAR DIARY
or
INTELLIGENCE SUMMARY.

(Erase heading not required.)

Hour, Date, Place.		Summary of Events and Information.	Remarks and references to Appendices
6.3.15	6.30 pm	Fired 2 Rds at our Infantry's request on snipers who were worrying our working parties.	
		66th Bty.	
	9.30 am	fired a few Rounds at enemy's pump where large quantities of water were being drawn out –	
	2.40 pm	Shelled likely O.P. of "pipsqueak" who was firing our O.P. (RITZ).	
	5.30 pm	Registered with one Section on observation post S11c 3.7.	
7.3.15		7th Bty.	
	12.50 pm	Considerable activity was observed near house M 34 d 9.5, apparently a working party – Barbed wire in front of this house –	
	3. pm	Registered trenches but observation difficult owing to weather Conditions	
	3.57 pm	a pipsqueak Battery from direction of BOIS DU BIEZ shelled angle of Rds S2 b 9.9. fired a few Rds at Target 21 in reply –	
		14th Bty.	
	8 am.	fired four Rounds on party of enemy carrying sacks from Communicating to fire trench	
	8.35 am	Fired 4 Rds at snipers in post S5c.	
	10.30 am	O.P. shelled from direction of distillery – Several Shell fell just behind house	
	1.30 pm	Fired 4 Rds on house. corner of road S11a – House set on fire by 30th How. Bty –	
	5 pm.	Five german shell fell 250x in front of Bty –	
		66th Bty. One Section having moved to new position on night of 6th –	
	8.30. to 10 am	Section registered on parts of trench –	
		a quiet day –	

Gulab Singh & Sons, Calcutta—No. 22 Army C.—5-8-14—1,07,000.

Instructions regarding War Diaries and Intelligence Summaries are contained in F. S. Regs., Part II, and the Staff Manual respectively. Title pages will be prepared in manuscript.

WAR DIARY

or

INTELLIGENCE SUMMARY.

(Erase heading not required.)

Army Form C. 2118.

Hour, Date, Place.	Summary of Events and Information.	Remarks and references to Appendices
8.3.15	7th Bty –	
	~~A strong wind~~	
	A quiet day for ~~the~~ both sides – Registered certain Targets – The effect of the strong wind was very marked when firing on Target of narrow front.	
6.35 am.	14th Bty – Fired at party carrying Sandbags in S 10 b –	
9.30 am.	Registered portion of trench to assist Infantry working party at night.	
10.50 am	Registered Communication trench –	
	66th Bty. Remaining two Sections came into new position on night of 7th	
	Registered allotted trenches –	
9.3.15	7th Bty –	
12 noon.	Fired 7 Rds. Registration – Result Satisfactory –	
7.30 am.	14th Bty – Fired a few Rounds at working party in Redoubt, S.10.b.	
2.30 pm	fired a few Rds and Verified trenches –	
3.45 pm	fired on party walking behind fire trench –	
	Reconnoitred line of advance across country & found practical –	
	Country much drier –	
10.30 am and 1. pm	66th Bty – fired on snipers in enemy's trenches as an Infantry working party was being worried by them –	
	The 7th + 66th forward of advance would have to be carried out along the road – The telephone wires of each Battery were very carefully examined today – IX Bde R.F.A. to be mobile Bde & ready to push on to advanced positions whenever required –	
	Wagon lines brought close up behind guns –	

Gulab Singh & Sons, Calcutta—No. 22 Army C.—5-8-14—1,07,000.

Instructions regarding War Diaries and Intelligence Summaries are contained in F. S. Regs., Part II, and the Staff Manual respectively. Title pages will be prepared in manuscript.

WAR DIARY
or
INTELLIGENCE SUMMARY.
(Erase heading not required.)

Army Form C. 2118.

Hour, Date, Place.	Summary of Events and Information.	Remarks and references to Appendices
9.3.15 –	About 8pm. received special order from General Sir D. Haig Commanding 1st Army – "We are about to engage the enemy under very favourable conditions, – – –. Reinforcements have made us stronger than the enemy in our front. – – – –. Our guns are now both more numerous than the enemys are, and also larger than any hitherto used by any army in the field – Our Flying Corps has driven the Germans from the air. – – – – – – – – – – – – – – – – –".	
10.3.15 – 6.32 to 6.45am.	Each Battery fired a few Rounds to ~~verify~~ verify Range + Corrector.	
7.30 am to 7.40 am	Each Battery fired as ordered – 1st Phase – 50 Rounds a gun at the wire in front of enemy's fire trench – Result very satisfactory – When Infantry advanced practically no wire to be seen –	
7.40 to 8.5 am	Each Battery turned their fire on to trenches allotted to them – and fired about 150 Rounds during the 2nd Phase – 25 minutes –	
8.5 am	Fire was turned on to Targets allotted – 3rd Phase – As our Infantry advanced — Slow Rate of Section fire –	
8.45 am	14th Bty – Observing officer reported fire trench taken as far as LA BASSEE Road – Many prisoners reported having been seen ~~[illegible]~~ –	
9.45 am	O.O. reported small reinforcements for the enemy coming up in S 5 c.	
11.30 am.	O.O. reported our Infantry at M visible – Range increased by 200x –	
1.35 pm	AUBERS CHURCH seen to be on fire –	

Gulab Singh & Sons, Calcutta—No. 22 Army C.—5-8-14—1,07,000.

Instructions regarding War Diaries and Intelligence Summaries are contained in F. S. Regs., Part II, and the Staff Manual respectively. Title pages will be prepared in manuscript.

WAR DIARY

or

INTELLIGENCE SUMMARY.

(Erase heading not required.)

Army Form C. 2118.

Hour, Date, Place.		Summary of Events and Information.	Remarks and references to Appendices.
10.3.15.	1.45 pm.	observing officer report in 'PORT ARTHUR' (cross roads S 4 d) reports enemy still holding about 100 yards of trench S 4 d 8 7.	MAP – FRANCE Sheet 36 S.W. 1/20000
	2.45 pm.	'Pipsqueak' shelled the O.P. so fired six Rounds at distillery S 17 a 'P' stopped	
	4.45 pm.	fired on ground behind Road S 6 d to support attack on BOIS DU BIEZ.	
		16th Bty –	
	10 a.m.	fired a few Rounds at enemy seen in trench about 100x E. of point N –	
	11am to 5 pm.	fired at various Targets as they presented themselves in area S 5 c	
	5.30 pm.	fired at Germans retreating in direction of S 11 a 8 8 (point M) –	
	1.30 to 4 pm.	Battery was shelled by a 4" Howitzer – no damage done – one Gunner wounded in leg – (one of observing party) – occasional Rounds fired during the night – on night lines –	
	7.19 pm.	14th Bty shelled road at S.E. corner of BOIS DU BIEZ – NEUVE CHAPELLE taken today – mostly ruins –	
11-3-15.	8.50 am.	7th Bty – fired on enemy's machine guns between S 5 d 9 9 & S 6 a 1 3.	
	9.56 –	fired on Germans massing on N.W. corner of BOIS DU BIEZ –	
	11.15 –	fired on German Counter attack (small) from the North end of B. DU B. observation officer reported fire very effective –	
		fired on Section of guns S.W. of S 6 a 7 8, which our O. officer located.	
	12.15 pm.	Heavy fire on allotted portion of Road – S 5 d 9 9 to S 6 a 1 3 –	
	2.8 to 2.12 pm 9.05 to 10 pm.	16th Bty – Heavy Infantry fire heard in direction of B. DU B. so opened fire on Road – at 7.4 – five minutes after the Signal S.O.S. D.D. (DEHRA DUN) was received – rate of fire increased – 10 pm all quiet again –	
	1.35 a.m.	outbursts of rifle fire for a few minutes – telephone wire cut – many breaks found –	

Army -

WAR DIARY
or
INTELLIGENCE SUMMARY.
(Erase heading not required.)

Instructions regarding War Diaries and Intelligence Summaries are contained in F. S. Regs., Part II, and the Staff Manual respectively. Title pages will be prepared in manuscript.

Hour, Date, Place.		Summary of Events and Information.	Remarks and references to Appendices.
11-3-15.	5am to 7am.	fired on line S5c 8.0 to S5a 10.3 with occasional bursts of fire –	
—	9.30 am.	a few Rounds gun fire behind. S11a 6.8 as enemy were reported there –	
	10.55 am	News of Counter attack on NEUVE CHAPELLE from N.W. corner of BOIS DU BIEZ,	
		switched Battery on & fired a few Rds gun fire –	
	2.8 to 2.12 pm	fired Rapid fire on allotted portion of road in front of BOIS DU BIEZ.	
		and then lifted fire to line 200x E of Eastern edge of B. DU B. –	
	3 pm.	our Infantry attacking Northern edge of B DU B – apparently successful –	
		wire to observing Station in 'PORT ARTHUR' constantly cut during	
	6 pm.	the day & repaired – Movement seen in Redoubt S10b, 4 Rounds fired into it –	
		10 pm. Shelled houses in vicinity of S17a – flashes visible among them –	
		66th Bty –	
	8.45 am	fired series of bursts of fire on enemys machine gun on N.W. edge of B. DU B. –	
	9.50 to 10 am.	Rapid fire on Germans assembling in front of our line –	
	11.10 am.	Fired on German Counter attack towards NEUVE CHAPELLE –	
	2.8 to 2.12.	Rapid fire on allotted portion of Road –	
	2.15 pm	Increased Range & continued for a short time with slow Rate of fire.	
	2 to 5 pm	Enemy dropped large number of 'Black Marias' in front of Battery	
		slight damage to two Gun epaulments – B.C. & Captain covered	
		with mud otherwise no damage –	
		2Lieut LOUGHRIDGE went from 7th Bty to MEERUT DIV. AMN. COLUMN –	
12-3-15 –		7th Bty. –	
	1.20 to 1.40 am	Heavy fire heard on our front so opened fire on night lines – firing ceased at 1.40 am –	
	6 am –	telephone wire broken but was soon mended again –	

Ninnik & Sons, Calcutta—No. 36 Army C.—20-8-14—1,500 Bks.

Instructions regarding War Diaries and Intelligence Summaries are contained in F. S. Regs., Part II, and the Staff Manual respectively. Title pages will be prepared in manuscript.

WAR DIARY
or
INTELLIGENCE SUMMARY.
(*Erase heading not required.*)

Army Form C. 2118.

Hour, Date, Place.	Summary of Events and Information.	Remarks and references to Appendices.
12.3.15 12.30 to 1 pm	Each Battery fired on front in front of BOIS DU BIEZ, the last five minutes at a rapid rate of fire – our Infantry were trying to reach the BOIS.	Each Battery.
1 pm to 1.10 pm	fired at longer Range into the BOIS – and then lengthened Range to form screen beyond the BOIS firing at a slow rate –	
	occasional Rounds were fired during the night –	
	16th Bty.	
5.17 pm	Heavy fire heard in direction of BOIS DU BIEZ – opened on night lines at slow rate	
2.6 pm	Fired at enemy in fire trench near LA BASSEE Road as snipers from there were worrying our Infantry on the left –	
	Reconnoitred advanced positions at M 33 b –	
5 pm	fired a few Rounds at digging party in front of BOIS –	
	fired a few Rounds during the night –	
	66th Bty.	
5.20 am	opened fire on night lines as heavy fire heard on our front – observation difficult all morning & situation hard to follow –	
12.10 pm	Fired on Germans in trenches near LA BASSEE Road –	
4.15 pm	Carefully registered enemy's trench S 5 6 9.0 where Germans were seen to enter –	
	Wagon line shelled this morning – one Horse killed – Wagon line moved about 200x S.E. –	
	Shells from "Pipsqueak" coming over Battery all afternoon – most of them falling in RICHEBOURG ST VAAST –	
5.30 to 8 pm	occasional Rounds were fired – on BOIS DU BIEZ –	

[illegible] Calcutta—No. 25 Army C—20-3-14—1,500 Bks.

Army Form C. 2118.

WAR DIARY
or
INTELLIGENCE SUMMARY.
(*Erase heading not required.*)

Instructions regarding War Diaries and Intelligence Summaries are contained in F. S. Regs., Part II, and the Staff Manual respectively. Title pages will be prepared in manuscript.

Hour, Date, Place.		Summary of Events and Information.	Remarks and references to Appendices.
13.3.15.	12 noon.	7th Bty – Registered enemy's trench S5637 – S5688	
	1 pm.	Fired on Section of enemys Battery in action S.W. of S6a 5.10. – The enemy's Battery stopped firing – one direct hit obtained, detachments seen running to cover – Range 4500x. Percussion Shrapnel –	
	3.40 pm.	Fired Rapid fire for one minute on Eastern edge of BOIS DU BIEZ where enemy were reported to be massing –	
		The observing Station has been under fire almost continuously during the day + communications interrupted many times by shell fire –	
	7 am.	14th Bty – Reconnaissance by obs. officer for better O.P.	
	7.15 –	O.P. established near Cross Roads N. of point D.	
	10 am.	German field Battery started shelling RUE DU BOIS + the O.P. from the direction of distillery – Searched the area of distillery with a few shell –	
	10.40 am	Germans seen going into house W. of BOIS DU BIEZ – Shelled the house in conjunction with 40th Howitzer Battery –	
	11 am	New O.P. destroyed by a German Shell –	
	2 pm.	Registered several points in rear of new German trenches W. of B.DU B. So as to take advantage of fleeting Targets –	
	3.40 pm	Fired at Road running into S of BOIS to disperse Germans reported to be massing there –	
	10.30 pm	Fired a Salvo on night lines –	
		66th Bty	
	1.55 pm	Registered points between S. end of B. DU B. and ESTAIRES – LA BASSEE Road.	
	3.40 pm	opened with rapid fire for one minute on Eastern Edge of BOIS DU BIEZ where enemy were reported to be massing –	
	3.50 pm	Repeated –	
	4.15 pm	Fired a few Rounds on trench on W. side of B.DU B.	
		Lieut DSC Evans R.G.A. from 66th Bty R.F.A. to No 5 Siege Bty R.G.A.	

Gulab Singh & Sons, Calcutta—No. 36 Army C.—29-8-14—1,500 Bks

Instructions regarding War Diaries and Intelligence Summaries are contained in F. S. Regs., Part II, and the Staff Manual respectively. Title pages will be prepared in manuscript.

WAR DIARY
or
INTELLIGENCE SUMMARY.

(Erase heading not required.)

Army Form C. 2118.

Hour, Date, Place.		Summary of Events and Information.	Remarks and references to Appendices.
14-3-15.	1.20am	7th Bty – on receipt of Signal S.O.S. D.D. The Battery opened fire on its	
—	2 am	night lines — stop firing ordered —	
	8.20am	Fired on enemys trench S5b3.7 to S5b3.8 to stop snipers working parties.	
		Bursts of fire were directed on this trench at intervals during the day –	
	10.20am	Fired at Section of enemys guns south of Cross Roads S6a5.9.	
	12.10pm	Lieut G. KIDDLE was wounded in the head while observing the	
		fire of the Battery from the O.P. S5a5.10. – wound slight.	
	6.20pm	Each Battery fired three Rounds rapid fire on night lines as enemy	
		were reported to be massing behind wood —	
		There was systematic shelling of the RUE DU BOIS this afternoon from the	
		RITZ to PORT ARTHUR. The Germans evidently mean to knock	
		down all possible OPs — The O.P. in NEUVE CHAPELLE was also	
		receiving much attention this morning —	
		14th Bty –	
	11.30am	Registered enemys trench in S11d + S11a –	
	11.20am	fired a few Rounds at working party in S11a + b —	
	12.noon	fired 2 Rounds at FERME DU BIEZ – S12c –	
	7.pm	Two Rounds fired at registered trench S11b – where working party seen before dark	
	8.50pm	Repeated above —	
		66th Bty –	
	9.15am	Registered two points of German trench West of BOIS DU BIEZ –	
	12.15pm	Registered on place where Infantry reported machine Gun —	
	12.35 –	Fired two Rounds at M. Gun – the second round very effective –	
		having knocked off the helmets of three Germans who were observing	
		with field glasses —	
	5.40pm	Observing Officer reported that his house was knocked down & that he was looking for another one —	

Gulab Singh & Sons, Calcutta—No. 30 Army C.—29-8-14—1,000 Bks

Army Form C. 2118.

Instructions regarding War Diaries and Intelligence Summaries are contained in F. S. Regs., Part II, and the Staff Manual respectively. Title pages will be prepared in manuscript.

WAR DIARY

or

INTELLIGENCE SUMMARY.

(Erase heading not required.)

Hour, Date, Place.	Summary of Events and Information.	Remarks and references to Appendices.
14-3-15. 6.10pm	fired a few Rounds on Germans crossing field behind trench in S11b –	
	Copy of memo from G.O.C. R A. Indian Army Corps dated 14-3-15 – The following remarks made by Sir JAMES WILLCOCKS Commanding the Indian Army Corps are forwarded for your information, and communication to those under your command –	
	" The invariable assistance given by the Artillery to our Infantry and the admirable manner in which all the Batteries were handled at NEUVE CHAPELLE only serve to prove that no Gunners equal British –	
	The Highest praise is due to the Divisional and Brigade Artillery Commanders and Staffs, and the splendid officers, N.C.O's and men of the Royal Artillery of the Corps –	
	The work of the officers and men of the Divisional Ammunition Column is always been of a high order —	
	The Above was Received on 15-3-15 –	
	IV Bde R.F.A. to be under C.R.A. LAHORE Divn — from 14.3.15 to ?	

Gulab Singh & Sons, Calcutta—No. 36 Army C.—29-8-14—1,500 Bks

Instructions regarding War Diaries and Intelligence Summaries are contained in F. S. Regs., Part II, and the Staff Manual respectively. Title pages will be prepared in manuscript.

WAR DIARY
or
INTELLIGENCE SUMMARY.

(Erase heading not required.)

Army Form C. 2118.

Hour, Date, Place.	Summary of Events and Information.	Remarks and references to Appendices.
15-3-15. 1.5am	7th Bty – Heavy rifle fire was heard on our front. 3 Rounds of gun fire were fired on night lines S5a89 – S6a12. – afterwards all quiet – The Battery now in support of the H.L.I. who are holding the left of the front occupied by SIRHIND BDE – The Battalion Hd Qrs are at my O.P. S5a5.10 –	7th Bty with H.L.I. No 4 Subsection 66th " " 4th Gurkhas 3 " 83rd " " 15 Sikhs 2 " 84th " " 1st Gurkhas 1 " Bde
7.37½am	14th Bty. Strong working party seen near house S11b2.6 – others seen arriving. Shelled working party in conjunction with 2nd Siege Battery R.G.A. – Some of them took refuge in house until it was destroyed when remaining men disappeared towards BOIS DU BIEZ followed by our Shrapnel –	14th & 55th Btys night lines on Cross Roads to the South –
10.58am	Mine Howitzer shell fell in front of Battery – Total damage, one aiming post knocked down –	
	66th Bty – Early in the morning a party was sent up to build up house which had been blown up yesterday but remainder of house collapsed & a new place found at S10a89.	
2.45 to 4pm –	Heavily shelled by "Black Marias" – about 60 shell fell between Battery and RICHEBOURG CHURCH – First shell killed four Battery horses & laid out 3 men of 4th London Regt – Telephone wires also cut –	
4.45pm	Telephone line to O.P. being mended registered on night lines – O.C. IV Bde Commander of Left Section (RA) IV Bde night lines from S5d16 to S5b710 – XI Bde Covers remainder of front – O.C. Right Section reports his night lines join with mine – Communication with Artillery of 8th Divn not yet joined up – will be done early to-morrow –	

Govt. Press, Calcutta – No. 30 Army C. –29-8-14 –1,500 Bks

Army Form C. 2118.

WAR DIARY

or

INTELLIGENCE SUMMARY.

(*Erase heading not required.*)

Instructions regarding War Diaries and Intelligence Summaries are contained in F. S. Regs., Part II, and the Staff Manual respectively. Title pages will be prepared in manuscript.

Hour, Date, Place.	Summary of Events and Information.	Remarks and references to Appendices.
16-3-15	7th Bty –	
12.10am	Heavy rifle fire heard on our left, but all quiet on our front – observation very difficult owing to mist – Nothing to report till dark –	
11.20pm	The Signal S.O.S. D received from H.L.I. Hd Qrs in N. CHAPELLE – The enemys Infantry having opened a very heavy rifle fire on the left front flank of our trenches – The Battery opened fire at once on night lines and the enemy immediately ceased firing –	
	14th Bty – This morning a new German trench has been started in the LA-BASSEE Road and has been runs about 300 yards towards the BOIS DU BIEZ –	
6.25am	fired on digging party near the 11 in S11 –	
6.40am	fired on working party behind barricade in LA.B. Road – Effect v. good –	
Between 7.45 + 10.3am	occasional Rounds fired whenever party started work –	
	66th Bty – Nothing to Report – every thing very quiet and observation difficult owing to mist –	
17-3-15.	7th Bty –	
10.45am	While RICHEBOURG was being shelled the Obs. officer located by their flashes 2 Heavy German Guns – Probable position near LA-CLIQUETERIE about T3a – Too far away to take on –	
	14th Bty –	
8.26am	fired a Salvo at Enemys Battery in S12a –	
8.30.	fired few Rounds at Enemys Battery in S17b.	
8.40	fired 3 Rounds at white house in S11b – several Germans seen coming from there –	

Army Form C. 2118.

WAR DIARY
or
INTELLIGENCE SUMMARY.
(Erase heading not required.)

Instructions regarding War Diaries and Intelligence Summaries are contained in F. S. Regs., Part II, and the Staff Manual respectively. Title pages will be prepared in manuscript.

Hour, Date, Place.		Summary of Events and Information.	Remarks and references to Appendices.
17.3.15	9.45am	Fired 3 Rounds at enemys trench immediately behind Barricade on LA BASSEE Road. Probably an O.P. as Germans were observed looking with glasses there. Observing station shelled heavily today.	
		Captain J.C. CROCKER joined Bde today (from ABBEVILLE) & posted to 14th Bty.	
		66th Bty. The enemy consistently shelled RICHEBOURG CHURCH and neighbourhood during the night about one Round every half hour.	
	Between 9am & 12 noon & 1.30pm & 3pm	RICHEBOURG again heavily shelled.	
18.3.15		A very quiet day. Observation difficult owing to mist.	
		7th Bty did not fire.	
	9.30am 12 noon	14th Bty. fired one round on working party in fire trench a few yards N. of LA BASSEE Road. Two men hit.	
	12 noon	Our O.P. shelled by "pipsqueak". 2 direct hits obtained on house but no one hurt. Many shells fell close to O.P. from direction of BOIS DU BIEZ.	
	7pm	2 Rds fired on Cross Roads S12 a.	
	8am	66th Bty. fired 3 Rds at Germans repairing Earthwork in S5c 6.9.	
19-3-15.		The JULLUNDUR BDE relieved the SIRHIND BDE. The relief being completed by 12 midnight 18/19 March.	7th Bty Manchesters [illegible]
		Left Section divided into three Subsections.	66th 4th Suffolks [illegible]
		7th Bty. Nothing to report. Observation very difficult today.	53 & 54 Bty 47th Sikhs [illegible]
		The following transfer took place today Temp Lieut Campbell Grant from 14th to [illegible] Lt C. Simmons from [illegible] to 14th Bty.	14th & 85th light lines [illegible]

Army Form C. 2118.

WAR DIARY
or
INTELLIGENCE SUMMARY.
(*Erase heading not required.*)

Instructions regarding War Diaries and Intelligence Summaries are contained in F. S. Regs., Part II, and the Staff Manual respectively. Title pages will be prepared in manuscript.

Hour, Date, Place.	Summary of Events and Information.	Remarks and references to Appendices.
19.3.15.	14th Bty – Nothing to Report till after 5 pm –	
5.45 pm	fired at working party in S11b –	
6.10 pm	fired at White house S11b 2.6. Germans seen coming from house –	
	66th Bty –	
	RICHEBOURG shelled at frequent intervals during the day with 'Black Marias' –	
2 pm –	Three direct hits were obtained on the Church –	
4.30 pm	fired 2 Rds at party of Germans at S5d 6.8 –	
20.3.15.	Temp Lieut E.C. Knight joined Bde and posted to 7th Bty –	
	7th Bty – Did not fire – nothing to report – although good day for observation –	
6.20 + 6.55 am	14th Bty – Fired at Snipers in S10b who were sniping at observation House a good deal –	
	fired at working party in White House S11b 2 6.	
7.20 am	Registered Pink House S11a 9.3. which was reported to be an O.P. –	
11.44 am	Shelled working party at S11b 2 6. White House – as continued activity there –	
2 pm.	Two Sausage balloons seen during the afternoon to S.W. –	
	66th Bty –	
8.30 am	Enemy's aeroplane seen – Nothing to Report except that a few Shell fell near the Battery this afternoon –	
21-3-15.	7th Bty.	
9.30 to 10.20 am	a Hostile Battery from S.W. Corner of BOIS DU BIEZ shelled NEUVE CHAPELLE – Battery could not be located –	
10.55 am	Hostile Battery shelled the O.Cs. O.P. –	

Gulab Singh & Sons, Calcutta.—No. 36 Army C.—29-8-14—1,500 Bks

Army Form C. 2118.

Instructions regarding War Diaries and Intelligence Summaries are contained in F. S. Regs., Part II, and the Staff Manual respectively. Title pages will be prepared in manuscript.

WAR DIARY
or
INTELLIGENCE SUMMARY.

(Erase heading not required.)

Hour, Date, Place.		Summary of Events and Information.	Remarks and references to Appendices.
21-3-15	5 pm	Registered house S5b9.1. where activity had been noticed. 3 direct hits obtained.	
	10.50 pm	O.C. Manchester Regt. reported great activity in German Communication trench S5b91 to S5b45. So fired 2 Rounds gun fire at trench – Infantry reported work stopped –	
		14th Bty –	
	11 am.	fired 2 Rds in direction of 'pipsqueak' in S12c & stopped their fire.	
	"	fired at working party in enemy's trench –	
		66th Bty –	
	12.15 pm	Nothing to report till just after noon when very heavy shell fell behind the Battery – not less than 11" – RICHEBOURG CHURCH	
	12.50 pm	being repeatedly hit and spire finally knocked off – Shelling promptly ceased –	
	3 pm.	fired 3 Rounds at enemy in trench along BOIS DU BIEZ –	
	5 pm.	Three heavy Howitzer shell fell in RICHEBOURG near wagon line – causing some Casualties amongst the H.L.I. and wounding one man of the Battery – the water cart being destroyed – These shell were probably observed by a German aeroplane which flew over at that time – Three bombs were dropped – one setting fire to a house – Our Anti aircraft guns seem to be too far away from trenches.	
22-3-15.		The following transfer took place – Capt D.C.G. RUTHERFOORD from 66th to 14th Battery – Capt J.C. CROCKER from 14th to 66th Battery –	

Army Form C. 2118.

Instructions regarding War Diaries and Intelligence Summaries are contained in F. S. Regs., Part II, and the Staff Manual respectively. Title pages will be prepared in manuscript.

WAR DIARY
or
INTELLIGENCE SUMMARY.

(*Erase heading not required.*)

Hour, Date, Place.	Summary of Events and Information.	Remarks and references to Appendices.
22.3.15. 4.30pm	7th Bty – Fired on German Communicating trench near Bridge M 36 c 1,3 where Germans were seen in considerable number – The Battery O.P. has been heavily shelled three times during the day by Battery somewhere S.E. of LIGNY LE PETIT –	
1 am	14th Bty – Heavy fire heard to the South in direction of LA QUINQUE RUE	
10 am	German aeroplane seen – very high up –	
11.35 "	Fired 4 Rds into FERME DU BIEZ as 'pipsqueak' was active –	
2.10pm	Fired 3 Rds at enemys trench S5c – Small party of Germans seen	
5.50 am	66th Bty. Moved four guns to new Battery position at M 33 a 0.4.	
7 am	Ready to fire + Communications Complete – Moved 3rd Section –	
8 am	fired a few Rounds to Register lines – O.O. had a rotten time today as pipsqueak was firing on his part of the trench at intervals + the enemy threw bombs in the afternoon – Aircraft guns still shooting very short –	
23-3-15.	Captain R.B. MILLER posted to Bde from 5th Division – 7th Battery – 7th Bty. No firing during the day – Enemy's Infantry on our front quiet – Their Artillery shelled NEUVE-CHAPELLE on three occasions –	

Army Form C. 2118.

Instructions regarding War Diaries and Intelligence Summaries are contained in F. S. Regs., Part II, and the Staff Manual respectively. Title pages will be prepared in manuscript.

WAR DIARY
or
INTELLIGENCE SUMMARY.
(Erase heading not required.)

Hour, Date, Place.	Summary of Events and Information.	Remarks and references to Appendices.
23-3-15. 12.45 pm	14th Bty – fired two Rounds at party of men carrying planks S.W. corner of BOIS DU BIEZ S11b83 – party dispersed –	
4.20 pm	fired at periscope in new Redoubt just E. of LA BASSEE Road –	
3.30 pm	66th Bty – fired at house at corner of BOIS-DU BIEZ reported to be occupied by the enemy –	
24-3-15. 4.45 pm	7th Bty – Nothing to Report during night and all quiet during morning – Considerable activity was observed in the German communication trench S5b9.1. to S5b4.5 – Two Rounds gun fire were fired at this Target which appeared very effective – Three men hit near O.P. today – two very slight –	
	14th Bty – 2/Lieut PARCELL and one man selected for course in Trench Mortar –	
6 am	dispersed working party S11b2.6 –	
9.41 am	fired on working party behind fire trench carrying planks –	
3.7 pm	fired 3 Rounds H.E. at wire near barricade – effect little better than P.S.	
9.40 am	66th Bty – fired on observation house of 'pipsqueak' who was firing on our trenches, one horse HQ on ~~IV~~ IV Bde hit at LA COUTURE –	
25-3-15 –	IV Bde came out of action before dawn to billets at RIEZ DU VINAGE – LAHORE DIV. relieved by 1st Division – III Bde ~~ammn~~ Am. Col. remaining at R19b –	

Army Form C. 2118.

Instructions regarding War Diaries and Intelligence Summaries are contained in F. S. Regs., Part II, and the Staff Manual respectively. Title pages will be prepared in manuscript.

WAR DIARY
or
INTELLIGENCE SUMMARY.
(*Erase heading not required.*)

Hour, Date, Place.	Summary of Events and Information.	Remarks and references to Appendices.
25-3-15-	all A.T. Carts sent to BERGUETTE – They are shortly to be sent to MARSEILLES for ? – G. S. Wagons received in their place –	
26-3-15-	Rest –	
27-3-15-	do.	
28-3-15-	do.	
29-3-15-	do –	
30-3-15-	do -	
31-3-15.	do.	

J Turnbull Capt.
Adj IV Bde R.F.A.

31/3/15

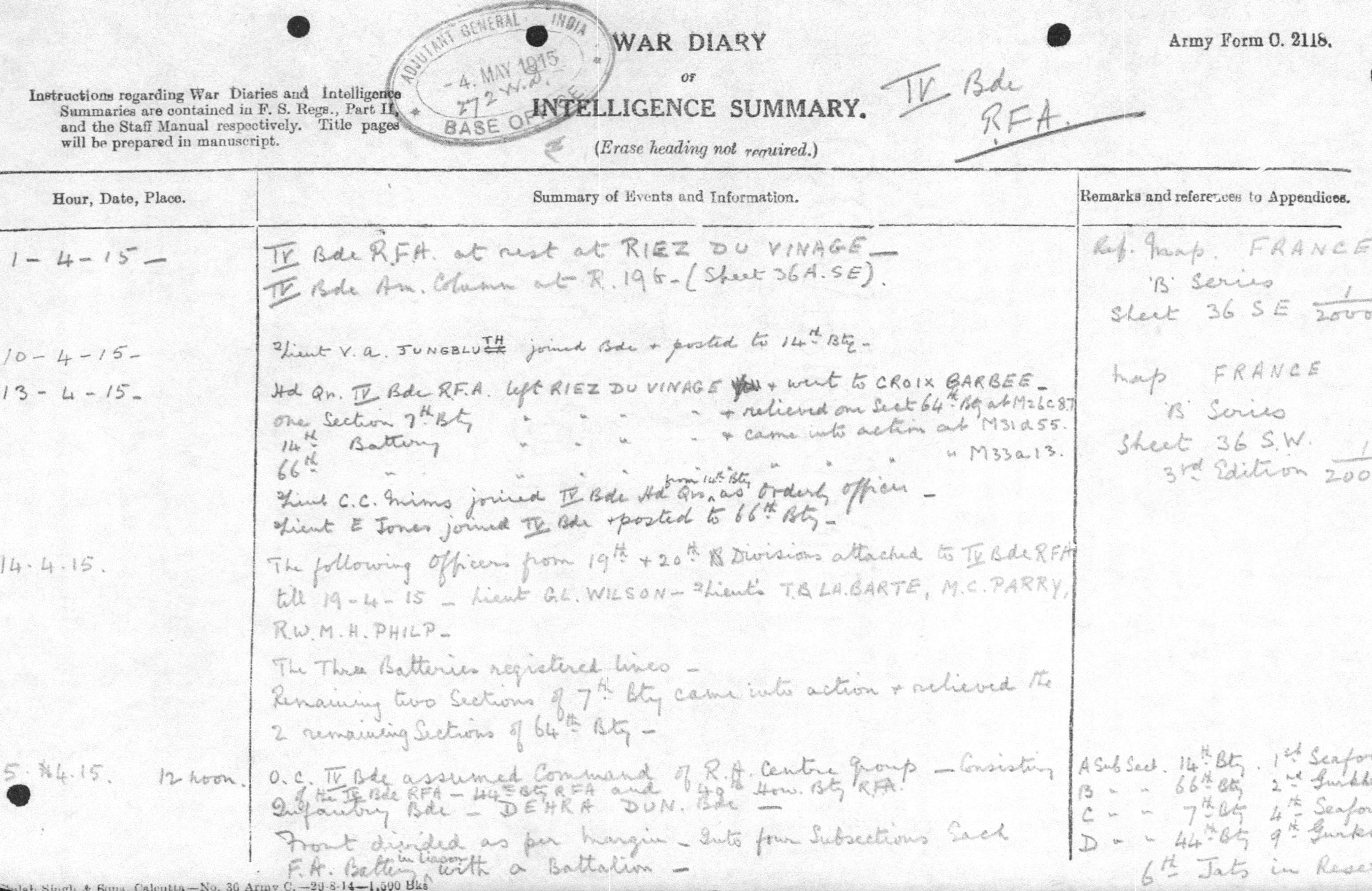

Instructions regarding War Diaries and Intelligence Summaries are contained in F. S. Regs., Part II, and the Staff Manual respectively. Title pages will be prepared in manuscript.

WAR DIARY
or
INTELLIGENCE SUMMARY.
(Erase heading not required.)

IV Bde R.F.A.

Army Form C. 2118.

Hour, Date, Place.	Summary of Events and Information.	Remarks and references to Appendices.
1-4-15 –	IV Bde R.F.A. at rest at RIEZ DU VINAGE – IV Bde Am. Column at R.19b – (Sheet 36A.SE).	Ref. Map. FRANCE 'B' Series Sheet 36 SE 1/20000
10-4-15 –	2/Lieut V. A. JUNGBLUTH joined Bde + posted to 14th Bty –	
13-4-15 –	Hd Qr. IV Bde R.F.A. left RIEZ DU VINAGE + went to CROIX BARBEE – One Section 7th Bty " " " " + relieved one Sect 64th Bty at M26c87 14th Battery " " " " + came into action at M31d55. 66th " " " " " " M33a13. Lieut C.C. Mims joined IV Bde Hd Qrs. from 14th Bty as Orderly Officer – 2/Lieut E Jones joined IV Bde + posted to 66th Bty –	Map FRANCE 'B' Series Sheet 36 S.W. 3rd Edition 1/20000
14.4.15.	The following Officers from 19th + 20th Divisions attached to IV Bde RFA till 19-4-15 – Lieut G.L. WILSON – 2/Lieuts T.B. LA.BARTE, M.C. PARRY, R.W.M.H. PHILP – The Three Batteries registered lines – Remaining two Sections of 7th Bty came into action + relieved the 2 remaining Sections of 64th Bty –	
15.4.15. 12 noon.	O.C. IV Bde assumed Command of R.A. Centre Group – Consisting of the IV Bde RFA – 44th Bty RFA and 43rd How. Bty RFA. Infantry Bde – DEHRA DUN. Bde – Front divided as per margin – Into four Subsections Each F.A. Battery in liaison with a Battalion –	A Sub Sect. 14th Bty 1st Seaforths – B " " 66th Bty 2nd Gurkha Rifles C " " 7th Bty 4th Seaforths – D " " 44th Bty 9th Gurkha Rifles 6th Jats in Reserve.

Instructions regarding War Diaries and Intelligence Summaries are contained in F. S. Regs., Part II, and the Staff Manual respectively. Title pages will be prepared in manuscript.

WAR DIARY
or
INTELLIGENCE SUMMARY.
(*Erase heading not required.*)

Army Form C. 2118.

Hour, Date, Place.		Summary of Events and Information.	Remarks and references to Appendices.
15.4.15. Contd.		A quiet day – very little doing – nothing of interest to Report – Each Battery fired a few Rounds to Register Certain points –	
16.4.15 –	9 am.	7th Bty – a quiet and nothing to report till 9 am when a German field Howitzer was observed shelling their own trenches – pt 128.	
	12 noon –	fired 3 Rounds at German trenches at pt 130 where activity seen –	
	1.5 pm	Battery observing House shelled – two direct hits – no one hurt –	
	4 pm	Observing House again shelled –	
		14th Bty. Hurdles were put down as platforms with Sandbags on top – Gun jumped slightly to the right first round – afterwards steady	
	8.30 am	66th Bty – Registered night lines along Bois Du Biez –	
	4.30 pm	House about 500x Right front of Battery shelled by pipsqueak	
17.4.15 –		A quiet night – nothing to Report – a few Rds were fired to Register certain points during day	
	6.45 am	German Battery fired eight rds at Brewery (one of our observing stations) at NEUVE CHAPELLE –	Bois Du Biez map 1/10000
	10.40 am	66th Bty fired at supposed machine gun emplacements near pt 130 –	

Gulab Singh & Sons, Calcutta – No. 36 Army C. – 29-8-14 – 1,500 Bks

Army Form C. 2118.

Instructions regarding War Diaries and Intelligence Summaries are contained in F. S. Regs., Part II, and the Staff Manual respectively. Title pages will be prepared in manuscript.

WAR DIARY
or
INTELLIGENCE SUMMARY.
(Erase heading not required.)

Hour, Date, Place.		Summary of Events and Information.	Remarks and references to Appendices.
17.4.15	11.15am	German field Howitzer firing over NEUVE CHAPELLE from behind BOIS-DU-BIEZ – Bty not located –	
	2. pm	German Bty shelled trenches of C Subsection – 7th Bty replied by firing on trenches opposite –	
	3.30 pm	House set alight just North of pt (64) – This house must have been a store for ammunition as explosion of rifle ammunition was heard for 17 minutes after house was well on fire –	
	12.15 pm 2. pm 3.30 pm	one of our Batteries fired on party of Germans who were very busy making 'dug outs' at pt (63)	
	4.50 pm	German How. Battery fired on Crescent trench – 14th Bty replied at firing at Battery supposed to be in S.17.a. – German Bty stopped firing –	
	5.40 pm	Enemy's Infantry from trenches on our front fired on our aeroplanes who were reconnoitring – our Batteries fired on German trenches with good effect –	
	7.50pm	Heavy transport heard on Road just this side North of	
	+ 10 pm	BOIS DU BIEZ – Two of our Batteries fired at different parts of this road ———	
	11.55pm	a good deal of rifle fire heard on our front –	

Army Form C. 2118.

WAR DIARY
or
INTELLIGENCE SUMMARY.
(*Erase heading not required.*)

Instructions regarding War Diaries and Intelligence Summaries are contained in F. S. Regs., Part II, and the Staff Manual respectively. Title pages will be prepared in manuscript.

Hour, Date, Place.	Summary of Events and Information.	Remarks and references to Appendices.
18.4.15.	a few Rounds were fired in early morning to Register certain points on enemy's trenches – a quiet night –	
9.5 am + 9.50 "	German aeroplanes firing light were fired on by our Infantry + Archibalds	
6.25 pm	Batteries fired on German trenches to keep down hostile fire on our aeroplane –	
	German Artillery very quiet today	
	Batteries fired on several working parties during the day otherwise nothing of interest to Report –	
19.4.15.	a few Rds were fired early to Register certain points. a good deal of musketry fire during night 18/19 —	
8.20 am + 3.15 pm	Brewery in NEUVE CHAPELLE (observing station of 66th Bty) Shelled + Bty telephone wires cut –	
	7th Bty O. S. also shelled –	
8.44 am	Pipsqueak active from S17a on our trenches – 14th Bty fired a few rounds on likely position –	
8.45 am	House near (12.5) fired on thought to be a likely Obs. Station	
9.45 am	" at S5d10.9 fired on —	
10.45 "	14th Bty Registered supposed Bty position near (V23)	VIOLAINES MAP 1/5000

Dulab Singh & Sons, Calcutta—No. 36 Army C.—29 8 14—1,500 Bks

Army Form C. 2118.

Instructions regarding War Diaries and Intelligence Summaries are contained in F. S. Regs., Part II, and the Staff Manual respectively. Title pages will be prepared in manuscript.

WAR DIARY
or
INTELLIGENCE SUMMARY.
(*Erase heading not required.*)

Hour, Date, Place.	Summary of Events and Information.	Remarks and references to Appendices.
19.4.15. 11.15 ~~11.05~~ am	tall poplars near pt. (46) Registered —	
11.30 am + 12.30 pm	Houses at (50) + (51) Registered —	
2.20 + 3.20 pm	66th fired on working parties near pt. (63)	
3.5 pm	Three good Rds by 16th Bty put into strong working party at S11b	
5.15 pm	A few Rds put into House S.W. of pt (125) where enemy were seen to be sniping from (by 7th Bty) — This point is evidently a strong one + Heavy Btys have been asked to fire at it —	
	No German aeroplanes seen today —	
	The four attached officers from 19th + 20th Divns left Bde for England —	
20/4/15.	A quiet night - a few Rounds fired to Register certain points in Enemy's trench in early morning —	
	Enemy shelled the Brewery (66th Bty O.P.) several times during the day — Major Crofton V. slightly wounded — Lieut Elles and a Gunner both wounded + sent to Hospital - not seriously —	
	7th Bty O.P. twice shelled today —	
3.35 pm	Enemy's snipers very active from house S.W. of pt (125) - 7th Bty fired a few Round at house + stopped them —	
1.43 pm to 2.15 pm	Enemy shelled ST VAAST and RICHEBOURG - about 25 shells.	
	The following objectives were fired on today —	

... & Sons, Calcutta — No. 36 Army C.—29-8-14—1,500 Bks

Army Form C. 2118.

WAR DIARY
or
INTELLIGENCE SUMMARY.
(Erase heading not required.)

Instructions regarding War Diaries and Intelligence Summaries are contained in F. S. Regs., Part II, and the Staff Manual respectively. Title pages will be prepared in manuscript.

Hour, Date, Place.		Summary of Events and Information.	Remarks and references to Appendices.
20.4.15.	9.45 am	14th Bty fired on trench just E of pt (53)	
—	11 am & 12 noon	House at pt (69) fired on by 40th How Bty & 66th Bty —	
	12.20 pm	7th Bty fired on large working party between (130) & (131) — good result.	
	12.55 pm	14th Bty Registered F.M.S. DU BIEZ.	
	4.15 pm	Fired at enemy's Infantry in trenches as they were firing on an aeroplane.	
	6.45 pm	Fired at enemy observed in house at pt (121) —	
21-4-15.		Each Battery fired a few Rounds to Register wire at pts in G. trenches.	
—	8.30 to 9.30 am	Enemy shelled houses (including 7th & 66th OPs) in NEUVE CHAPELLE with 5.9 – 4.2 Howitzers & pipsqueak and also at other times during the day. —	
		The following objectives were fired at today —	
	5.30 am	Houses near point (51) where party of Germans were seen.	
	8.45 "	at Enemy's Infantry who were watching German shell falling in NEUVE CHAPELLE —	
	2.25 pm	66th fired 14 Rounds in Co-operation with 60 pounder guns on Houses at points (124) & (126) —	
	3.57 pm	Germans in trench near pt (51) —	
	5.20 pm	14th Bty fired on house (R16) —	
	6.30 pm	at Enemy's Infantry who were firing at our aeroplane —	

G. I. Pub. Sch. & Sons, Calcutta—No. 30 Army C.—29-8-14—1,500 Bks.

Instructions regarding War Diaries and Intelligence Summaries are contained in F. S. Regs., Part II, and the Staff Manual respectively. Title pages will be prepared in manuscript.

WAR DIARY

or

INTELLIGENCE SUMMARY.

(*Erase heading not required.*)

Army Form C. 2118.

Hour, Date, Place.	Summary of Events and Information.	Remarks and references to Appendices.
7 pm.	~~[illegible]~~ Two effective Rounds were fired at a party of about 20 Germans in S11b –	
about 9 pm.	One Section of 14th and 44th Batteries changed places, the remainder of the Batteries to change places tomorrow night — Observing Officers of both Batteries visited the O.P.'s of the other Battery today –	
22.4.15.	A quiet night except for heavy rifle fire between 3 + 4 am on our left –	
	Early this morning each Battery fired a few Rounds at wire in front of enemy's trenches –	
	Enemy fired at intervals at Brewery and surroundings with heavy shell and pipsqueak –	
9.5 am	14th Bty fired at party of men (observers) looking over trench S11b –	
	Various trenches and a few houses (O.P.'s) were fired on –	
about 6 pm	Flashes observed at N26c6.5. –	
	Observing Officer 66th Bty observed for 108th H. Battery firing on house in front of BOIS DU BIEZ – (German O.P.)	
about 8.30 pm.	The remainder of 14th + 44th Batteries changed places –	
	German Battery shelled their own trenches today pt	(56)

Army Form C. 2118.

WAR DIARY

or

INTELLIGENCE SUMMARY.

(Erase heading not required.)

Instructions regarding War Diaries and Intelligence Summaries are contained in F. S. Regs., Part II, and the Staff Manual respectively. Title pages will be prepared in manuscript.

Hour, Date, Place.	Summary of Events and Information.	Remarks and references to Appendices.
23.4.15.	Early in the morning each Battery fired a few Rounds at wire –	
10.48 am	77 millimeter Battery fire a few Rounds at 66th O.P. and Infantry trenches in front of it – 66th fired a few Rds at O.P. at pt. (69). Very few Rds fired into NEUVE CHAPELLE today –	
3.15 pm	7th Bty fired a few Rounds at movement in house at pt. (63).	
	A quiet day	
	Each Battery reconnoitred positions about R 29 – late in the evening –	
24.4.15.	Night of 23/24 very quiet – Each Battery fired a few Rounds at certain points on enemys wire – Only a few Rounds were put into NEUVE CHAPELLE district. The following objectives were taken on today –	
9 to 9.30 am	a few Rounds fired on Germans in trenches who were firing at our aeroplane –	
12.6 pm	7th Bty fired a few Rounds at pt (129) –	
12.50 pm	14th – Registered from pts (140) to (204)	
4 pm	" " fire trench in front of pt. (66) & fired on working party in communicating trench –	
4.15 pm	(48) taken on by Heavy Battery and one field Battery to beg runners. The strong wind made ranging very difficult today –	

Instructions regarding War Diaries and Intelligence Summaries are contained in F. S. Regs., Part II, and the Staff Manual respectively. Title pages will be prepared in manuscript.

WAR DIARY
or
INTELLIGENCE SUMMARY.

(*Erase heading not required.*)

Army Form C. 2118.

Hour, Date, Place.	Summary of Events and Information.	Remarks and references to Appendices.
25.4.15	On the night of the 24/25 April the 40th How. Battery came out of action + went North – One Section of 30th How. Battery took over night lines on points in front of 'C' + 'D' Subsections – The 2nd Siege Bty R.G.A. with four guns were laid on night lines on 'A' + 'B' Subsections – A quiet night – Each Battery Registered early in the morning at enemy's wire –	
11 am –	66th Bty fired on house point 63 –	
11.45 –	7th Bty fired on party of men observed in Communicating trench near pt 65	
Between 12 + 2 pm.	Enemy fired 10.5 cm. into Brewery + neighbourhood from Ht POMMEREAU.	
3.30 pm.	Observing Officer observed for 24th H. Battery at houses along BOIS-DU-BIEZ –	
4 pm	14th Bty Registered House M36d 2.7 and House pt 122 – Two hits –	
	Very little going on today –	
	2 Lieut A.A.D. KEMPSTER (Special Reserve) joined the Brigade from IPSWICH and posted to 66th Battery –	
26.4.15	A very quiet night – Very misty in the morning till about 8.30 am when a few Rounds were fired on wire in front of trenches –	
	2 Lieut J. BAINES joined IV Bde from IPSWICH (Temp Com.) posted to 7th Bty	
	2 Lieut M. THORESBY-JONES " " " " " " " 14th Bty –	

Army Form C. 2118.

Instructions regarding War Diaries and Intelligence Summaries are contained in F. S. Regs., Part II, and the Staff Manual respectively. Title pages will be prepared in manuscript.

WAR DIARY
or
INTELLIGENCE SUMMARY.
(Erase heading not required.)

Hour, Date, Place.	Summary of Events and Information.	Remarks and references to Appendices.
11.20 am.	7th Bty fired on House 60x SW of 125 where Infantry reported Snipers active	
11.30 am	16th " fired on Houses 123 + 124 – Infantry Co-operated with rifle fire –	
12.5 pm.	66th " " on Sandbag emplacement near 130 –	
12.45 pm	" " " " House 66 and on trench in front of it –	
2.30 pm	" " " " " 69 –	
3.5 pm	7th " " Enemy's O.P. pt 65 – Three hits on house –	
3.40 pm	66th " " on Barricade at pt 133 –	
6.20 pm	Heavy fire from German trenches at our aeroplane which was flying very low down – Our Batteries fired on trenches to keep rifle fire down –	
6.15 – 7 pm	Enemy shelled 66th O.P. and NEUVE CHAPELLE with Heavy Howitzer – 66th Responded by firing on German trenches – At the Same time The Black Watch Salient was bombed – 66th Bty wire broken but soon mended again –	'E' Subsection.
27-4-15.	A quiet night – a few Rounds fired early on wire – A large hose pipe seen over parapet at pt. 131 – Two others seen 50x apart near pt. 66 – Infantry Report having heard water being pumped in German trenches – Enemy has continued working in front of 44th Bty at pt 57 – further Sandbags appear to have been added to parapet at this point –	

Gulab Singh & Sons, Calcutta – No. 36 Army C. – 29-8-14 – 1,500 Bks.

Army Form C. 2118.

Instructions regarding War Diaries and Intelligence Summaries are contained in F. S. Regs., Part II, and the Staff Manual respectively. Title pages will be prepared in manuscript.

WAR DIARY
or
INTELLIGENCE SUMMARY.

(Erase heading not required.)

Hour, Date, Place.	Summary of Events and Information.	Remarks and references to Appendices.
12.10 pm –	66th Bty Registered pt. 52 –	
12.30 pm –	14th – fired 2 Rds at House 100x S of 151 –	
1. pm –	3 shell fell near 14th Bty position at junction of Road M26a –	
1.15 pm –	6 Rds from enemy's field gun from S.E. direction on pt M34G34.	
1.50 pm.	Enemy's 4" Gun fired on Reserve trenches in rear of NEUVE CHAPELLE –	
4. pm.	14th fired on House at Cross Roads near pt. 125 –	
4.20 pm.	7th fired a few Rds on Snipers in German trenches –	
5.45 pm.	66th fired on pt. 69 –	
28-4-15 –	A quiet night – a few Rds were fired early on wire –	
8.42 am –	Enemy shelled NEUVE CHAPELLE with guns & pipsqueak – 14th Bty fired a few Rds at German trench near pt 140 in retaliation –	
9.30 – 11 to 11am + at 12.30 –	Enemy's 'pipsqueak' active near Gurkha Hd Qrs from N edge of BOIS DU BIEZ –	
10.45 am	66th Bty fired a few Rds on German trenches at pt 130 –	
11.20 –	" " " " " on trench at L in BRULOT –	
3.45 pm	14th Bty fired on House 100x S.W. of pt 151 – There is a hay stack close to the house with obviously a dug out underneath it – and destroyed it – (10 Rds)	
6.5 pm	66th fired on hose pipe at pt 131	
6.15 pm	7th Bty fired 16 Rds on the two hose pipes near pt 66 – Direct hits obtained on the parapet at both points –	

Instructions regarding War Diaries and Intelligence Summaries are contained in F. S. Regs., Part II, and the Staff Manual respectively. Title pages will be prepared in manuscript.

WAR DIARY

or

INTELLIGENCE SUMMARY.

(*Erase heading not required.*)

Army Form C. 2118.

Hour, Date, Place.	Summary of Events and Information.	Remarks and references to Appendices.
29-4-15	On the night of the 27-28 and 29-30 April – The GARHWAL Bde relieved the DEHRA-DUN Bde — Our front [illegible] A quiet night on our front — Early in the morning a few Rounds were fired at wire in front of German trenches. 7th Bty O.P. was shelled three times during the day – Several direct hits on the house –	A Subsection [illegible]
		B. " 2/8 Gurkhas [illegible]
		C. " Garhwal Rifles [illegible]
		D. " 2/3 Gurkhas [illegible]
9.25–9.45am	Hostile aeroplane over NEUVE CHAPELLE – was fired at by [illegible]	
11.15am	20th Bty fired a few rounds at snipers in houses [illegible] latter were seen to be on fire about ten minutes later.	
11.55am	[illegible] fired on house at [illegible] where Infantry reported snipers & a machine gun —	
4.30pm	10th fired on house 100x S.W. of 131, with lyddite [illegible] a dugout close by —	
4.45pm	[illegible] fired some few rounds at snipers in house [illegible] Much warmer today – Horse rugs sent away today – To be 'done up' for next winter —	
30-4-15	A quiet night — Misty morning but cleared about 8 am – a warm day — At pt. 131 – a permanent gap in wire entanglement – Germans were mending wire near this pt. last night –	

Army Form C. 2118.

WAR DIARY
or
INTELLIGENCE SUMMARY.
(Erase heading not required.)

Instructions regarding War Diaries and Intelligence Summaries are contained in F. S. Regs., Part II, and the Staff Manual respectively. Title pages will be prepared in manuscript.

Hour, Date, Place.	Summary of Events and Information.	Remarks and references to Appendices.
	Our O.P's in NEUVE CHAPELLE are rapidly being made untenable	
11.25am	7th Bty fired a few Rds at Snipers —	
11.40am	a German biplane flying high passed over Batteries flying WEST — Archibalds fired on him but did no good — a few Rounds were fired at Houses which contained Snipers —	
6pm.	14th + 66th fired at Germans in trenches who were firing on our Aeroplane —	
	Lieut. B A H. GAGE, 7th Bty, awarded Military Cross — Also two men in 7th Bty the D. C M —	
30-4-15	[signature] Capt. Adj IV Bde RA.	

38.

IV. Brigade R. F. A.

1st May 31st May

Instructions regarding War Diaries and Intelligence Summaries are contained in F. S. Regs., Part II, and the Staff Manual respectively. Title pages will be prepared in manuscript.

WAR DIARY IV Bde RFA
or
INTELLIGENCE SUMMARY.
(Erase heading not required.)

Army Form C. 2118.

Hour, Date, Place.	Summary of Events and Information.	Remarks and references to Appendices.
1.5.15 4.20 am	A quiet night till 4.20 am when Enemy started a Heavy Bombardment on NEUVE CHAPELLE – PORT ARTHUR and along the RUE DU BOIS – The bombardment was heavier from P.A. to the West – our Batteries replied by shelling the enemy's trenches and probable O P's for about 1¼ hours – The Germans were evidently expecting us to attack as most of their shell fell behind our trenches and along Roads behind – Some good shooting was done to parapets of trenches and a good deal of damage done – German aeroplanes were up frequently today –	FRANCE map. Sheet 36 SW 3rd Edition – 1/20000
10.30 am	66th O.P. was shelled by field Howitzer –	BOIS DU BIEZ map. 1/10,000 –
10.50 –	66th fired at 'L' Shaped House at 125 which was Reported as an O.P.	
11. am	7th Bty O.P. hit by five Heavy shell –	
11.20 –	7th Bty fired a few shots into German O.P. at 63 –	
2.5.15.	A quiet night – Each Bty fired a few Rounds at wire early –	
7.45 am	Light Howitzer shelled ground in front of 14th Bty position –	
9.	14th Bty Registered Salient between 137–141 –	
2.20 pm and 11.20 am	66th fired on working party in Redoubt N of 63 –	
11.55 and 6.30 pm	14th fired on house 124 – probably O.P. as men were seen entering House –	

Army Form C. 2118.

Instructions regarding War Diaries and Intelligence Summaries are contained in F. S. Regs., Part II, and the Staff Manual respectively. Title pages will be prepared in manuscript.

WAR DIARY
or
INTELLIGENCE SUMMARY.
(*Erase heading not required.*)

Hour, Date, Place.	Summary of Events and Information.	Remarks and references to Appendices.
12. noon	Enemy shelled NEUVE CHAPELLE and trenches in front of it – 7th and 66th Btys replied by shelling enemy's trenches & probable OPs –	
7.30 pm	14th fired a few Rounds on Road 121 – 118 with hope of catching reliefs.	
3.5.15	A quiet night – Batteries fired on wire in early morning –	
1 pm	Trenches on the Right of 'A' Subsection heavily bombed –	
2.54	66th Bty fired on trenches near 133 where movement was seen –	
6 pm	German biplane over our trenches – It was fired on by our Infantry and 'Archies' –	
6.27 pm	Batteries fired a few Rounds to stop Infantry firing on our Aeroplane.	
4.5.15	A quiet night again – Same procedure on wire –	
11.20 am	66th fired on party leaving house at 51 –	
4.45 pm	14th fired at working party carrying planks in support trench near 138 – This party was kept busy for some time trying to retrieve planks which they had hurriedly dropped –	
	An extremely quiet day –	
5.5.15	Another quite night – Rds again fired at wire early –	
6 am	pipsqueak had 2 direct hits on 7th OP out of 6 shots –	
10.20	14th fired at point 191 – (Register) –	

Instructions regarding War Diaries and Intelligence Summaries are contained in F. S. Regs., Part II, and the Staff Manual respectively. Title pages will be prepared in manuscript.

WAR DIARY
or
INTELLIGENCE SUMMARY.

(Erase heading not required.)

Army Form C. 2118.

Hour, Date, Place.	Summary of Events and Information.	Remarks and references to Appendices.
2.5 pm & 4pm	7th Bty fired on working party near 131 –	
2.7 pm	14th " " " " " 151 –	
5.40 pm.	7th fired a few Rounds at House 125 where Infantry Snipers were very active –	
	The following F.A. Subalterns attached to IV Bde today for 14 days instruction – W.A.D. EDWARDS (to 7th Bty) – W.F. YOUNG (to 14th Bty) F.R. BAKER (to 66th Bty).	
	The JULLUNDER Bde Relieved GARHWAL Bde to right – and took over line as per margin –	A Subsection 4th Suffolks (44th Bty) B " & 57th Rifles } 40th Pathans } 66 Bty C " 59th Rifles 7th D " 1st Manchesters 14th
6-5-15 –	Another quiet night – and a very misty morning till 9 am – near 57 the enemy have strengthened their trenches last night –	
5 am.	light Howitzer shelled ground in front of 14th Bty position about 6 Rounds –––	
	during the morning Pipsqueak & 5.9" shelled our support trenches (& Communicating) in rear of RUE DU BOIS. Various tasks being ordered – Batteries registered them today –	
6 pm.	14th Bty Registered large shields, probably machine gun shields – near pt 128 –	

Army Form C. 2118.

Instructions regarding War Diaries and Intelligence Summaries are contained in F. S. Regs., Part II, and the Staff Manual respectively. Title pages will be prepared in manuscript.

WAR DIARY
or
INTELLIGENCE SUMMARY.
(*Erase heading not required.*)

Hour, Date, Place.	Summary of Events and Information.	Remarks and references to Appendices.
	Lieut W.F. YOUNG from 14th Bty ordered to join attached to No 1 Group Heavy Artillery	
7.5.15	fairly quiet night – morning misty till about 8 am.	
	Each Battery Registered 'certain' points during the day – 'All ready' –	
1.20 pm.	Pipsqueak shelled 7th OP scoring 2 direct hits –	
1.10 & 3.10 pm –	14th fired on working party in Enemys communicating trench –	
3 pm –	Two Batteries fired on enemy's trenches to keep down rifle fire on our aeroplane –	
	7th Bty had 6 direct hits on Fme DU BIEZ.	
4 pm	66th Bty O.O. assisted 28th Bty to Register –	
7.45 pm	14th fired 6 Rds at working party near 128.	
8.5.15	a quiet night – Each Bty fired a few Rds on wire Early.	
8.20 am	German Bty over NEUVE CHAPELLE – taken on by our Archies – & flew off –	
9.30 –	14th Fired on Houses 123 & 124 where sniping was coming from	
11.10 –	66th Had one direct hit on Fme DU BIEZ –	

Army Form C. 2118.

Instructions regarding War Diaries and Intelligence Summaries are contained in F. S. Regs., Part II, and the Staff Manual respectively. Title pages will be prepared in manuscript.

WAR DIARY
or
INTELLIGENCE SUMMARY.

(Erase heading not required.)

Hour, Date, Place.	Summary of Events and Information.	Remarks and references to Appendices.
4.30 pm	14th fired on House 140 where Infantry had located Machine Gun in House – M.G. located in large hole in lower half of wall of House, apparently at N.E. Corner – During Registration smoke of discharge of machine Gun observed – 6 Rounds H.E. ~~[illegible]~~ fired – Three detonated properly – 2 on German wire – This was cut but the iron posts supporting it was not knocked down –	
6.45 pm	66th Bty fired 3 Rds at working party at S11 b 22 –	
9.5.15. about 4.45 am	Batteries fired a few Rounds to Register and find 'Corrector of day' –	
	R.A. LAHORE Batteries told off to cut wire – IV Bde Batteries to	
[illegible]	Keep down enemys fire on trenches on left of where ~~attack~~ the Infantry attack was to be delivered –	
5 am	Batteries opened fire on their ~~various~~ allotted trenches – phase I + fire was kept up till phase IV.	
5.42 –	Our Infantry seen advancing from PORT ARTHUR –	
7.55 –	fire was again started on phase I as evidently the Infantry had been held up – (by machine Guns) – Very little fire from the (enemys) trenches in front of our Batteries and only one machine Gun seen which the 66th fired on + silenced –	
3.20 pm	fire was again started on phase I to 4 pm –	
	During the night of 9/10 each Battery fired at intervals on communicating trenches + roads leading to them –	

Army Form C. 2118.

Instructions regarding War Diaries and Intelligence Summaries are contained in F. S. Regs., Part II, and the Staff Manual respectively. Title pages will be prepared in manuscript.

WAR DIARY
or
INTELLIGENCE SUMMARY.
(Erase heading not required.)

Hour, Date, Place.		Summary of Events and Information.	Remarks and references to Appendices.
10.5.15	4.30 am	Enemy's Howitzer shelled ground in front of 14th Bty position – no damage done at all –	
	5.15 am	German aeroplane over NEUVE CHAPELLE but driven back by 'Archie'	
	11.30 am	Pipsqueak had four direct hits on 7th Bty O.P. –	
	4.10 pm	14th fired on House 120 + trench in front of it where men were seen –	
		7th Bty observing officer located about 12 galvanised iron tanks (?) on HILL side near HAUTE POMMEREAU – They appeared to be circular + about 4 to 5 feet in diameter – The tanks are placed along a trench, plainly visible, little trouble appears to have been taken to conceal them –	
	7.45 pm	14th Bty fired on working party at 130 –	
11-5-15	6.30 am	14th fired at working party at 127 – 7th Bty fired at party of men at 130	
	9.50 am	Heavy Howitzer shelled NEUVE CHAPELLE (from Brewery to M35c34)	
	2.45 pm	14th fired at groups of men behind fire trench at 145 146 –	
		Light Howitzer shelled LA BASSEE Road N.E. of 14th position at frequent intervals during the day –	
	about 11.20 am	DEHRA DUN Hd. Quarters ~~at~~ House had two direct on it today – They left for ~~an~~ a more healthy spot!	

Instructions regarding War Diaries and Intelligence Summaries are contained in F. S. Regs., Part II, and the Staff Manual respectively. Title pages will be prepared in manuscript.

WAR DIARY
or
INTELLIGENCE SUMMARY.
(*Erase heading not required.*)

Army Form C. 2118

Hour, Date, Place.	Summary of Events and Information.	Remarks and references to Appendices.
8.30 pm.	14th Bty fired at House 140 in Combination with Heavies —	
12-5-15 —	a quiet night — Morning misty till 7 a.m.	
2.30 pm.	14th fired at house 151 when party were seen to enter and also on working party behind enemy's trench near 146 — Nothing much to Report today — a few Rounds were fired at working parties & O.P's — a good deal of Hostile shelling of our Reserve trenches —	
13-5-15 —	Another quiet night — Very misty morning and not clear to observe till 8 a.m. — Each Battery assisted 1st Highland Bde Batteries to Register certain points on our front — Certain points were Registered during the day & specially Selected points were fired on along Enemy's wire — 9th O.P again shelled by pipsqueak & German heavy Howitzer shelled our trenches (support) —	
12 midnight 13/14-5-15 →	A good deal of fire from Batteries of our Division & the Division on our Right —	
13.5.15 10.5 pm —	14th Bty fired 2 Salvos on enemy's trench to keep down rifle fire near 128	
14.5.15 1 am —	IV Bde Batteries fired from 1.5 am to 1.7 am on German trenches from pt 65 to 133 — 45 Rds per Bty —	

Army Form C. 2118.

Instructions regarding War Diaries and Intelligence Summaries are contained in F. S. Regs., Part II, and the Staff Manual respectively. Title pages will be prepared in manuscript.

WAR DIARY
or
INTELLIGENCE SUMMARY.
(*Erase heading not required.*)

Hour, Date, Place.	Summary of Events and Information.	Remarks and references to Appendices.
2.5 pm	The above repeated –	
	During the afternoon the 66th O.P. was shelled by Heavy Howitzer – 12 Rounds of which 3 were direct ~~st~~ hits –	
8pm to 4am 15.5.15 –	7th + 66th Btys fired 6 Rds per hour on allotted tasks – (a Salvo of 2 guns every 20 minutes) –	
14.5.15 –	2/Lieut ~~F.~~ FRASER ordered to join 13th Bde RFA from 14th Battery – He left this afternoon –	
7.20 pm	Enemy's aeroplane seen by 14th Bty signallers stealing silently along our lines flying N.	
15.5.15.	2 Lieut G.A. WOLFERSTON (Temp. Commission) joined Bde today and posted to 14th Bty –	
	7th + 66th Batteries fired as ordered during the night –	
6.40am to 7.50am	Enemy bombarded front trenches of C Subsection with Howitzer + Pipsqueak –	
	The front of JULLUNDER Bde (four Subsections) is still the same but our Batteries have changed Subsections (in margin) –	A Subsection 66th Bty B " 7th Bty – C " 14th Bty D " 3rd Highland Bty –
	The 1st Highland Bde RFA. have been placed under us – Some new wire had to be laid so that Batteries could get into telephonic Communication with their new liaison Battalion –	The other two Highland Batteries have their lines in front of BOIS DU BIEZ –
11am –	14th Bty position was shelled by 6 or 8" Howitzer from direction of HT POMMEREAU – 12 shell fell near the Bty (3 blind) – one shell fell between number 3 and four gun and another very close to telephonists – no damage done – The fuse ~~off~~ one of one shell marked 42 Kz Gr Z 14 MA 15.	

Army Form C. 2118.

WAR DIARY

or

INTELLIGENCE SUMMARY.

(*Erase heading not required.*)

Instructions regarding War Diaries and Intelligence Summaries are contained in F. S. Regs., Part II, and the Staff Manual respectively. Title pages will be prepared in manuscript.

Hour, Date, Place.	Summary of Events and Information.	Remarks and references to Appendices.
4 pm.	66th Bty fired on Machine Gun emplacements near 56 – 2 direct hits obtained –	
6.20 pm	66th – fired on German trenches to keep down rifle fire on our Aeroplane –	
	1st Highland Bde Registered to day + did some good shooting – Double House, probable O.P., S.W. of 125 was hit and set on fire by one of their Batteries –	
8pm – 11.30 8pm.	Each Bty fired 8 Rds per hour at allotted tasks	
11.30 to 4.5.3	Fire was increased to 25 Rds per Bty –	
16-5-15 4.55 am –	Stop fire was given as the GARHWAL attack on our right had failed + the Infantry back again in their trenches –	
3.30 am	Three white Rockets observed, the first at 3.30 and the other two just after at one minute interval – These Rockets meant the the 20th (or 22nd?) Bde 7th Divisions attack had been successful.	
6 am.	14th Bty shelled O.P. at 121 – movement seen near this house –	
8.5 –	German Heavy Howitzer Bty shell the British trenches S. of PORT ARTHUR –	
9.10 –	14th Bty fired at Hostile Bty's near 118 and behind 117–147 –	
9.40 –	15 cm Howitzer shelled 7th Bty position – no damage –	
11.30 –	7th Bty fired on Suspected O.P. just W of 68 –	
11. –	14th " " " O.P. near 125 – 3 direct hits –	
2.45 + 5 pm	7th Bty fired on RED HOUSE – 160 – which was suspected as being an O.P. as one or two Huns were seen close by –	

Army Form C. 2118.

Instructions regarding War Diaries and Intelligence Summaries are contained in F. S. Regs., Part II, and the Staff Manual respectively. Title pages will be prepared in manuscript.

WAR DIARY
or
INTELLIGENCE SUMMARY.

(Erase heading not required.)

Hour, Date, Place.	Summary of Events and Information.	Remarks and references to Appendices.
3.43 pm –	16th fired on trees near 69 as Infantry reported sniper there –	
5.45 pm –	7th fired on German trenches to keep down rifle fire on our aeroplane –	
17-5-15 8.30-10.30pm	– Each battery fired on its night lines at the half hours –	
12.30-3.30am	Repeated –	
	2nd Lieut PARCELL left 16th Battery today & went to 1st Division – 'Bomb guns' –	
	During the day the enemy shelled line, RUE DU BOIS – PORT ARTHUR – NEUVE CHAPELLE – Their fire was kept nearly all day but most of their shell fell behind our trenches –	
	A Slow Rate of fire was kept up during the day on trenches and likely O.P's –	
9-10.30am	Several pipsqueaks fell near 66th B.G. –	
10.10 am	16th fired a few Rounds at enemy's pipsqueak near 118-119 –	
12.30 pm.	66th had 6 direct hits on House 50 – Reported to be an O.P.	
	During the day 7th B.G. fired on three occasions on House 160 as movement was seen –	
8.30pm-3.30am	Same procedure as last night –	
18-5-15. 7.30am	Slow Rate of fire opened & kept up during the day –	
4 pm –	fire increased to Section fire one minute	
4.20 pm	" " " " " 30" –	
4.30 pm	" reduced to 30 Rds an hour –	
	(The above rates of fire were ordered – evidently as a 'blind' –	

Army Form C. 2118.

Instructions regarding War Diaries and Intelligence Summaries are contained in F. S. Regs., Part II, and the Staff Manual respectively. Title pages will be prepared in manuscript.

WAR DIARY
or
INTELLIGENCE SUMMARY.
(*Erase heading not required.*)

Hour, Date, Place.	Summary of Events and Information.	Remarks and references to Appendices.
	Very little activity on the part of enemys guns during the day – during the night each Bty fired 6 or 8 Rds every hour to keep enemy alert –	
⊠	During the night 18/19 FEROZEPORE Bde relieved JULLUNDUR Bde	A ~~4th~~ Subsection 4th Londons B " 9th Bhopals C " 129th Baluchis D " Connaught Rangers
19-5-15.	A quiet day – on our front –	
2.45 pm	A Pipsqueak Battery shelled 7th Bty O.P.	
3.30 pm	14th Bty fired a few Rounds at House 100x S.W. of 125 – probable O.P.	
4.45 pm	66th had two good rounds into working party S11a 5.4.	
5.45 – 6.15 pm	Pipsqueak Bty put several shell near 66th Bty – no damage –	
20-5-15 –	A quiet night and very misty morning (early)	
7.15 am	Pipsqueak Bty active from near 147 – 14th Bty fired a few Rounds at his probable O.P. and at 147 as well –	
10.45 am –	66th fired four Rounds at working party near 51 –	
11.45 am	Light seen (probably Signalling lamp) in Roof of House W of 151 – 14th Bty fired a few Rounds at the house & got 2 direct hits –	
12 noon –	7th Bty fired 8 Rounds into Communication trench where movement was seen –	

Instructions regarding War Diaries and Intelligence Summaries are contained in F. S. Regs., Part II, and the Staff Manual respectively. Title pages will be prepared in manuscript.

WAR DIARY

or

INTELLIGENCE SUMMARY.

(*Erase heading not required.*)

Army Form C. 2118.

Hour, Date, Place.	Summary of Events and Information.	Remarks and references to Appendices.
from 1 pm.	a slow Rate of fire was kept up on enemy's trenches and a few hits obtained on probable O.Ps —	
1.25 pm.	a German aeroplane flew over NEUVE CHAPELLE but was driven back by our 'Archies' —	
2 – 5 pm.	14th Bty fired at Battery near 75 at intervals —	
6.55 pm.	a Pipsqueak Bty shelled 7th O.P. —	
10.10 pm.	German Heavy Howitzer shelled NEUVE CHAPELLE and vicinity of 7th O.P. —	
21.5.15.	1st Highland Bde told to stop firing as they have only 3000 Rds of ammunition left — none in D.A.C or Park —	
	1st Highland Bde went out of action in the evening. The line which they held on our front ~~was~~ taken over by altering lines of IV Bde to cover the whole of FEROZEPORE front —	
12 noon.	about 30 shells of various kinds fell near 14th Bty position — a large proportion blind —	
12.55 pm.	House between 65 and 68 fired on by 7th Battery as party of men were seen to enter it — Six direct hits obtained —	

Army Form C. 2118.

Instructions regarding War Diaries and Intelligence Summaries are contained in F. S. Regs., Part II, and the Staff Manual respectively. Title pages will be prepared in manuscript.

WAR DIARY
or
INTELLIGENCE SUMMARY.
(Erase heading not required.)

Hour, Date, Place.	Summary of Events and Information.	Remarks and references to Appendices.
3.15 pm.	Infantry reported house at S5d 43 to be an O.P. So 66th fired Eight Rounds at it – a slow Rate of fire was maintained on our front during the day –	
10 - 10.28 pm.	Rate of fire on our front quickened up to Section fire 1 minute	
10 - 28 - 10.30pm	+ to Section fire 30 Seconds – This was ordered by LAHORE DIV. – to try to make the enemy believe we were going to attack on our front + so draw men from from the South where an attack was going to be made later –	
22-5-15 –	a quiet night + morning –	
4.10pm	7th fired a few Rounds into House 60 yards S.W. of 125 from which the enemy were suspected of Sniping at 7th Bty O.P. –	
4.30pm.	14th Battery fired a few Rounds at Small party at X Roads near pt. 125 –	
	Lieut H.A. CUTLER – R.A.M.C. (temp Com.) joined the Bde today to take Capt. A.F.B. JONES' place as Medical Officer in Charge IV Bde R.F.A.	
10 pm.	German Heavy Howitzer shelled 7th Bty O.P. –	

Army Form C. 2118.

Instructions regarding War Diaries and Intelligence Summaries are contained in F. S. Regs., Part II, and the Staff Manual respectively. Title pages will be prepared in manuscript.

WAR DIARY
or
INTELLIGENCE SUMMARY.
(*Erase heading not required.*)

Hour, Date, Place.	Summary of Events and Information.	Remarks and references to Appendices.
23.5.15 – 12.30 pm	A quiet night and nothing to Report before noon –	
→	Enemy's Howitzer shelled Brewery – a few blind shell fell near 7th O.P.	
12.30 pm	14th fired on House 50x SW of 151 – Two direct hits – Signalling been going on there.	
3.45 to 4 pm.	Enemy shelled Road near 7th Bty – 7th + 66th fired a few Rds on trenches [illegible]	
6.20 pm.	66th fired a few Rounds on working party near 54 –	
24.5.15.	Another quiet night –	
11.15 am.	Enemy again seen Signalling at House near 151 – 14th Bty had 5 direct hits on House – (2 with H.E.).	
12 noon	I. Bde RFA. took over line from this morning – They having Registered and used our O.P.s yesterday – our observing officers withdrawn.	
9 pm. 23-5-15	Two Sections of 14th + 66th Came out of action and went back to their Wagon lines – The remaining guns The remaining guns were	
[illegible]	The same to come out at same hour on 24th –	
7 pm 24.5.15.	Received orders to Reconnoitre new positions for the Bde near RICHEBOURG and to occupy them with one Section during the night of 25/26. The Sections to Register on 26th + remaining Sections to come into action on the night 26/27 –	
	No definite task for Bde – direction RUE DU MARAIS – The Bde to remain in observation after Registration completed	
25.5.15 –	Positions Reconnoitred – + chosen S.E. of RICHEBOURG – The	

Army Form C. 2118.

Instructions regarding War Diaries and Intelligence Summaries are contained in F. S. Regs., Part II, and the Staff Manual respectively. Title pages will be prepared in manuscript.

WAR DIARY
or
INTELLIGENCE SUMMARY.

(*Erase heading not required.*)

Hour, Date, Place.	Summary of Events and Information.	Remarks and references to Appendices.
	Three Batteries being fairly close together –	
10 pm –	one Section of 7th + 66th came into action –	
26.5.15 – 3 am	one Section of 14th Bty came into action –	
	7th Bty S2c35 – 14th S2c94 – 66th S2d42 –	
	Each Battery Registered a few points during the day –	
3 pm to 4 pm.	7th Bty O.P., the "RITZ" shelled by Heavy Howitzers –	
27-5-15	LIEUT GATES transferred from IV Bde A.C. to 66th Bty.	
	2LIEUT E. JONES " " 66th Bty to IV Bde A.C.	
2 pm to 3 pm	RITZ Heavily shelled from direction of LORGIES –	
	LIEUT B.A.H. GAGE severely wounded by shell which struck a tree (high up) just behind the Bty – He was sitting on the ground with his Major at the time –	
12.30 pm.	Two Gunners 14th Bty wounded –	
28.5.15 –	Nothing to Report except that a few Rounds were fired to Register certain points –	
8.15 pm.	Enemy shelled RICHEBOURG with Heavy Howitzers setting fire to large House S. of Church –	
29.5.15 –	LIEUT B.A.H. GAGE promoted Temp Capt. 28.5.15 –	

Instructions regarding War Diaries and Intelligence Summaries are contained in F. S. Regs., Part II, and the Staff Manual respectively. Title pages will be prepared in manuscript.

WAR DIARY

or

INTELLIGENCE SUMMARY.

(Erase heading not required.)

Army Form C. 2118.

Hour, Date, Place.	Summary of Events and Information.	Remarks and references to Appendices.
6.30 am.	LIEUT G.A.H. ~~GE~~ GAGE died of wounds at VIEILLE CHAPELLE – (He received the Military Cross for very good work, at NEUVE CHAPELLE on March 10th and following days –	
6 pm –	He was buried at ST VAAST cemetery at Nearly all officers of Bde present and a large number of men from his Battery – (7th) – Brig Gen. LECKY (C.R.A. MEERUT DIV and his orderly officer LIEUT McFARLAN also present – PARDRÉ – Rev IRWIN – – Bearers LIEUTS KIDDLE, BEALL (7th Bty) JUNGBLUTH (14th Bty) OLIVER JONES (66th Bty) –	
	Each Battery registered a few points – observation difficult owing to heat haze –	
5.50 pm.	RICHEBOURG shelled by pipsqueaks –	
30-5-15 –	LIEUT CAMPBELL GRANT ordered to join LAHORE DIV. ARTY – He was posted to 93rd Bty R.F.A.	
	A quiet day – Batteries waited for aeroplane to arrive, to register certain points but owing to bad day it didn't come –	
	14th Bty had 4 direct hits on House S23 c 8.8.	
31-5-15 – 9.30 am	Heavy Howitzer Battery shelled RICHEBOURG CHURCH –	
	Early in the morning R.F. Corps' operator fixed station near 14th Bty – Wireless messages from German aeroplane intercepted by him – The	

Army Form C. 2118.

WAR DIARY
or
INTELLIGENCE SUMMARY.
(*Erase heading not required.*)

Instructions regarding War Diaries and Intelligence Summaries are contained in F. S. Regs., Part II, and the Staff Manual respectively. Title pages will be prepared in manuscript.

Hour, Date, Place.	Summary of Events and Information.	Remarks and references to Appendices.
	Aeroplane was observing fire for German Bty firing on ST VAAST and RICHEBOURG –	
6 pm.	114th Bty fired on K17 to L12 with assistance from aeroplane –	
7 pm	Small How Shell fell near RICHEBOURG CHURCH –	
From 6 AM –	The 8th, 49th (WEST RIDING), LAHORE and MEERUT DIVISIONS form INDIAN CORPS –	
	2.6.15.	
	Turnbull Capt Adj IV Bde RFA.	

IV Brigade R.F.A.

1st June 30th [illegible]

Instructions regarding War Diaries and Intelligence Summaries are contained in F. S. Regs., Part II, and the Staff Manual respectively. Title pages will be prepared in manuscript.

WAR DIARY
or
INTELLIGENCE SUMMARY.
(Erase heading not required.)

IV Bde RFA.

JUNE –

Army Form C. 2118.

Hour, Date, Place.	Summary of Events and Information.	Remarks and references to Appendices.
1.6.15. 4.30 am.	14th Bty Registered new trench J15 – K7 – also pts K6 and J12 –	Trench Map –
	Bursts of fire on this trench maintained throughout the day –	
6. am.	66th Bty Registered the following points with assistance of aeroplane.	
	S28a 42 – L17 – 29C 5.5.	
	7th Bty Registered K8 – J18 – also ends of trench in Eastern side of A36 –	
8 am –	14th Bty's O.P. shelled and abandoned	
9 to 10 am	Neighbourhood of 14th Bty (front) shelled by pipsqueak –	
	66th Bty Registered M13 – M11 –	
2.6.15.	14th Bty Kept up fire till 4.30 pm.	
	2Lieut M. THORESBY-JONES made a personal reconnaissance of trenches L8 – I2 – Good + useful report –	
	The following officers attached to Bde from to day for 14 days –	
	Brev. LIEUT COL. D.I.V. EATON – RCHA – (IV Bde Hd Qrs) –	
	Major G.L. WALKER – 2 LANCS Bty (T) (14th Bty) –	
	Lieut B.K. RONALD – (7th Bty)	
3.6.15 –		
9.20 – 10.20 am.	German aeroplane up observing –	
11.20 – 11.45 –	Enemy's 4.2 Howitzer shelled Road just W of 7th Bty –	

Army Form C. 2118.

Instructions regarding War Diaries and Intelligence Summaries are contained in F. S. Regs., Part II, and the Staff Manual respectively. Title pages will be prepared in manuscript.

WAR DIARY
or
INTELLIGENCE SUMMARY.
(Erase heading not required.)

Hour, Date, Place.	Summary of Events and Information.	Remarks and references to Appendices.
4 pm to 5 pm and 5.10 pm to 6 pm	Each Battery fired 50 Rounds on tasks at request of IV CORPS on our Right –	
7 pm to 9.40 pm	above Repeated –	
10 pm to 3 am	14th + 66th fired 10 Rounds an hour on same Targets –	
4.6.15 –		
about 12.40 pm	LIEUT R. D. BEALL killed by a shell which fell in his 'dug out' – one man 7th Bty wounded (slightly).	
6 pm	LIEUT BEALL buried at ST. VAAST close to LIEUT (Temp Capt) B. A. H. GAGE – Bearers – Lieuts KIDDLE, KNIGHT, 7th Bty – PRITCHARD, 14th Bty – MARSON, 66th Bty – Padre – Rev. IRWIN – nearly all officers of Bde present Brigade Major RA Meerut Div – there too –	
5.6.15 –	Nothing of any interest to Report –	
10.30 pm	One Section 7th Bty occupied position S8c 10.1. –	
6.6.15 –	Each Battery Registered a few points – LIASON with Batteries and Battalions established	

Army Form C. 2118.

Instructions regarding War Diaries and Intelligence Summaries are contained in F. S. Regs., Part II, and the Staff Manual respectively. Title pages will be prepared in manuscript.

WAR DIARY
or
INTELLIGENCE SUMMARY.
(Erase heading not required.)

Hour, Date, Place.	Summary of Events and Information.	Remarks and references to Appendices.
	today – Also IV Bde Hd Qrs in Communication with BAREILLY Bde and 2nd HIGHLAND Bde RFA –	
	This afternoon IV Bde took over front of BAREILLY Bde in place of IX Bde RFA who went to 7th Div –	
	13th Bde RFA on our left –	
	BAREILLY Bde ~~consists~~ of in trenches as per margin	A Subsection 41st DOGRAS 1 Coy 1/4 BLACK WATCH. 1 Coy 69th PUNJABIS –
	7th + 14th Bty with 'A' Subsection	B Subsection 1/4 B.W. less 1 Coy 1 Coy 69th P –
	66th with 'B' " –	
4.35 pm + 5.15 pm + 6.15 pm –	14th fired 6 Rds on enemy's trenches in retaliation to Germans shelling our trenches –	
about 5.30 pm	14th + 66th fired fired at the "Runners" when MOTHER fired on Q12 –	
11 pm –	Remaining two Sections of 7th Bty occupied new position	
7.6.15. 8. am + 11.25 am	66th fired on trenches near COUR D'AVOINE in retaliation to enemy shelling our trenches –	
9.45 to 10.45 am	Enemy's pipsqueak searched up to 50x of 7th Bty position –	
10.12 am –	14th fired, in retaliation, on German trenches –	

Instructions regarding War Diaries and Intelligence Summaries are contained in F. S. Regs., Part II, and the Staff Manual respectively. Title pages will be prepared in manuscript.

WAR DIARY
or
INTELLIGENCE SUMMARY.
(Erase heading not required.)

Army Form C. 2118.

Hour, Date, Place.	Summary of Events and Information.	Remarks and references to Appendices.
10.45 am	Pipsqueak hit 14th O.P. and house close to O.P. –	
12.30 pm –	14th fired at working party near P14 –	
4.15 pm –	66th Registered trench S28a29 – S28a99 –	
	7th Bty Registered several points during the day	
5 pm –	7th Bty attempted Registration by lamp with aeroplane. Conditions very difficult – no result obtained –	
8.6.15 6.30 am –	Pipsqueak shelled ground in front of 14th + 66th Btys – Observation very difficult today – A few Rounds were fired to Register – a few Rounds fired on German trenches in Retaliation to Germans shelling our trenches –	
9.6.15 12.55 am –	14th fired a few Rounds at bomb gun W of P14 at request from Infantry –	
4.15 am	German aeroplane up over 7th O.P. –	
8.45 am	Two German Reconnoitring aeroplanes up over 66th Bty – one plane dropped two lights over one of the Highland Bde Batteries – This H. Bde Bty had a few rounds put into them soon after –	
1.50 + 3.20 pm	Pipsqueak active on roads near 14th Bty –	

Army Form C. 2118.

. Instructions regarding War Diaries and Intelligence Summaries are contained in F. S. Regs., Part II, and the Staff Manual respectively. Title pages will be prepared in manuscript.

WAR DIARY
or
INTELLIGENCE SUMMARY.

(Erase heading not required.)

Hour, Date, Place.	Summary of Events and Information.	Remarks and references to Appendices.
11.45 am.	14th fired a few Rds at working party near Q8.	
4.3 pm.	Light Howitzer shelled RICHEBOURG –	
10.6.15.	A very misty day – Nothing of interest to Report –	
	a few Rds were fired at intervals on German trenches in retaliation to Germans shelling our trenches –	
11-6-15.	A Repetition of the 10th –	
12.6.15 – 9.10 am.	14th O.P. shelled by pipsqueak –	
12.35 pm.	14th fired on trench 100x SW of P14 – Explosion in trench one second after burst of shell – likely some bombs exploding –	
4. pm.	66th fired off a few Rounds at House near P16 where 3 Huns were seen to enter –	
5pm & 5.20 pm.	German aeroplane came over Batteries from direction of AUBERS.	
	During the day the enemy shelled our trenches at intervals, about 50% of shell blind – our Batteries replied by shelling German trenches – Observation Easy today –	
13.6.15	The Sand bagged house S.E. of P18 was fired on three times during the day when pipsqueak & Howitzers shelled our trenches – Shelling ceased at once each time – Asked for	

Army Form C. 2118.

Instructions regarding War Diaries and Intelligence Summaries are contained in F. S. Regs., Part II. and the Staff Manual respectively. Title pages will be prepared in manuscript.

WAR DIARY
or
INTELLIGENCE SUMMARY.
(Erase heading not required.)

Hour, Date, Place	Summary of Events and Information	Remarks and References to Appendices
	Heavy Artillery to take this house on —	
8.30 & 8.40 am	Two German aeroplanes up – evidently observing fire —	
10-30 am –	Heavy Howitzer shelled new tram line (South part) – KINGS Road to DEAD COW FARM —	
4 pm –	16th fired on M13 & M14 in retaliation to German shelling our trenches –	
14-6-15 –	a Colder day – from 50 to 100x had to be added to Ranges – a few Rounds fired on German trenches when Germans shelled our trenches —	
8.20 am	Enemys trench mortars fired on A Subsection Support trenches – all blind —	
9.15 am	Enemy's Howitzer, probably 5.9 – shelled 7th Bty orchard O.P. – direction LA BASSEE —	
1.30 pm	Light Howitzer & Pipsqueak shelling Road between Windy Corner and ST VAAST —	
5.50 pm	66th Bty fired 4 Rounds at enemy's working party S.E. of L17 —	

(9 29 6) W 2794 100,000 8/14 H W V Forms/C. 2118/11.

Army Form C. 2118.

Instructions regarding War Diaries and Intelligence Summaries are contained in F. S. Regs., Part II. and the Staff Manual respectively. Title pages will be prepared in manuscript.

WAR DIARY
or
INTELLIGENCE SUMMARY.
(Erase heading not required.)

Hour, Date, Place	Summary of Events and Information	Remarks and References to Appendices
	During the night 66th Bty fired a few Rounds, at request from Infantry, at working party near Q11 –	
15.6.15 11am.	Pipsqueak fired a few Rounds round about 7th Bty O.P.	
12.30pm	14th fired at Working party W of P14 –	
3.20pm	66th Shelled Sand bagged House S of Q12 in retaliation to Germans shelling our trenches N of Q7 –	
3.40 to 4.30pm.	German 5.9 ~~and~~ shelled CROIX BARBEE and fields NW of Cross Roads – There were a few remarks from here "where did that one go" –	
	During the afternoon enemy shelled Road N of Windy Corner.	
6.10pm.	Enemy shelled between 66th position and RUE de BERCEAUX.	
6.15pm.	66th fired a few Rounds in Retaliation to Germans firing on trenches of 'B' Subsection –	
8.45 to 11.15 pm	Heavy Howitzer, 8", shelled a little short of 14th Bty + close to 7th Mess from direction of ILLIES –	
16.5.16	A quiet night – Misty morning – observation difficult till 8 am.	

Instructions regarding War Diaries and Intelligence Summaries are contained in F. S. Regs., Part II. and the Staff Manual respectively. Title pages will be prepared in manuscript.

WAR DIARY
or
INTELLIGENCE SUMMARY.
(Erase heading not required.)

Army Form C. 2118.

Hour, Date, Place	Summary of Events and Information	Remarks and References to Appendices
2.35 pm.	66th fired at trenches S of P17 in Retaliation to Heavy Howitzers shelling our Reserve trenches –	
3.15 pm to 5.30 pm.	7th Bty fired at trenches L12 to 200x E.N.E. of L12 in accordance with instructions received – 7th were a few minutes late in starting owing to two breaks in wire –	
3.18 pm to 6 pm	14th & 66th fired a few Rounds at trenches in Retaliation –	
17-6-15.	A quiet night	
	German aeroplanes up early and again between 5.30 pm & 6 pm –	
11.50 am.	German Howitzer shelled close to our Hd Quarters – One shell fell four yards from House wounding two Gunners (TYLER & DILLON) and wrecking two bicycles –	
4.15 pm.	14th fired a few Rounds in Conjunction with 60 Pr. shelling P14 –	
	A few Rounds were fired at trenches in Retaliation to Germans shelling our trenches – 7th Bty leant to 9th Bde for Special job –	× A Subsection } – 6th JATS & 2nd SEAFORTHS
17/18-6-15 –	During the night DEHRA DUN Bde× relieved BAREILLY Bde –	B – } –
18-6-15 –	A quiet night –	A 7th & 14th – B 66th Btys –

(9 29 6) W 5794 10,000 8/14 H W V Forms/C. 2118/11.

Army Form C. 2118.

Instructions regarding War Diaries and Intelligence Summaries are contained in F. S. Regs., Part II. and the Staff Manual respectively. Title pages will be prepared in manuscript.

WAR DIARY
or
INTELLIGENCE SUMMARY.

(Erase heading not required.)

Hour, Date, Place	Summary of Events and Information	Remarks and References to Appendices
7.42 am –	A Cold morning – 125x to add at 4000x – 14th Registered M12 –	
8.50 am –	66th fired at Sand bagged House S of P17 in conjunction with 60 Pr.	
11.45 am –	14th Registered X14, 16, 19, 20 – as they are to fire on these trenches tonight	
1.47 pm.	66th Repeated –	
5.25 pm.	German reconnoitring plane up over RITZ, probably observing for 8"	
	How shelling area near old Highland Bty position –	
5.30 – 6.45 pm	Same aeroplane probably observing for Bty shelling RUE DE CHAVATTE near where 3 French Batteries are	
6.15 pm	14th fired on working party 70x S.W. of P14 –	
about 7.15 pm	7th Bty came back from being under orders of IX Bde R.F.A.	
19-6-15	Late on the night 18/19 – orders received for 14th to change on to trench further W –	
3.30 - 3.40 am	14th Bombarded trench X16 to Z3 with H.E. and Shrapnel –	90 Rounds fired –
3.43 - 3.53 am	" Searched 300x with Shrapnel –	
3.53 - 4 am	– Resumed on trench with H.E. and Shrapnel & then stopped firing	
	The above Bombardment was asked for by IV Corps –	
	They were having a feint attack –	
7.15 am	66th fired on Sand bagged House S of P17 in Retaliation to enemy shelling our trenches –	

Instructions regarding War Diaries and Intelligence Summaries are contained in F. S. Regs., Part II. and the Staff Manual respectively. Title pages will be prepared in manuscript.

WAR DIARY
or
INTELLIGENCE SUMMARY.
(Erase heading not required.)

Army Form C. 2118.

Hour, Date, Place		Summary of Events and Information	Remarks and References to Appendices
		This was repeated on three occasions –	
	12 Noon –	14th fired in Retaliation on trenches S.W. of P14 –	
	10.5 am.	Heavy Howitzer Bty shelled PRINCES ROAD just N of 7th O.P. –	
	6.15 pm.	The 7th Bty fired a few Rounds to Register night lines – (Having Returned from being under O.C. IX Bde –).	
	7.35 pm.	66th fired 6 Rounds at working party in Trench S.W. of Q12 –	
20.6.15.	5.30 am	14th fired at M12 & P14 in Retaliation for 77mm shelling our trenches.	
	9.55 am	66th fired at Sandbagged House " " Howitzer " " "	
	12 Noon –	14th fired at M20 – a gun firing from near there –	
2.20 &	3.15 pm	7th fired at Houses near P14 at request of Infantry who reported snipers there	
	2.45 pm.	14th fired at Same Houses to stop sniping –	
	4.45 pm.	14th Registered House just W of M23 – 77mm thought to be firing from near there on ST VAAST – RITZ Road – firing stopped at once –	
5.50 pm & 6.20 pm		German aeroplane up on left & front of Batteries –	
21.6.15.	5.15 am	66th fired 4 Rounds at Sandbagged House S. of P17 in retaliation to 77mm firing on our trenches – 77 stopped at once –	

(B 29 6) W 2794 100,000 8/14 H W V Forms/C. 2118/11.

Army Form C. 2118.

Instructions regarding War Diaries and Intelligence Summaries are contained in F. S. Regs., Part II. and the Staff Manual respectively. Title pages will be prepared in manuscript.

WAR DIARY
or
INTELLIGENCE SUMMARY.
(Erase heading not required.)

Hour, Date, Place	Summary of Events and Information	Remarks and References to Appendices
7.40 to 8.40 am	German aeroplane up – evidently observing fire –	
9.50 am + 12 noon	German Heavy Howitzer, 8", shelled QUEEN MARY ROAD – one direct hit on house S2 c 33. –	
5.45 pm.	7th Bty fired a few Rds at trenches near P14 at Request of Infantry.	
8 am to 9.30 am	Enemy's 5.9 shelled Road M27 d and Road running N.W – Two houses set on fire –	
5.45 to 7 pm.	Enemy's 5.9 shelled trenches S of CROIX BARBEE + vicinity of 'Archibald' – German aeroplane evidently observing fire.	
[illegible] 7.40 pm	14th fired at working party in trench SW of P14 – Party ran away.	
8 pm –	This was repeated at another party –	
	A quiet night –	
22.6.15 – 8.30 am.	Howitzer shelled N. corner of RICHEBOURG –	
9.30 am.	" " S. " " " –	
10.15 am.	77 mm firing from direction of M23 on fork of Road S7b – 14th Retaliated on M23 + behind M26 – 77 stopped –	
about. 7 pm.	IX Bde R.F.A. took over line from us – our observing parties withdrawn –	

Instructions regarding War Diaries and Intelligence Summaries are contained in F. S. Regs., Part II. and the Staff Manual respectively. Title pages will be prepared in manuscript.

WAR DIARY
or
INTELLIGENCE SUMMARY.
(Erase heading not required.)

Army Form C. 2118.

Hour, Date, Place	Summary of Events and Information	Remarks and References to Appendices
10 pm –	66th [illegible] [illegible] [illegible] [illegible] [illegible] [illegible] [illegible]	
[illegible] pm	[illegible]	
11 pm –	7th [illegible]	
23-6-15 – 8 [illegible]	IV [illegible] [illegible] [illegible] left [illegible] [illegible], [illegible] [illegible] [illegible], for ST FLORIS –	
24-6-15 –	Rest –	

[illegible]

Army Form C. 2118.

Instructions regarding War Diaries and Intelligence Summaries are contained in F. S. Regs., Part II. and the Staff Manual respectively. Title pages will be prepared in manuscript.

WAR DIARY
or
INTELLIGENCE SUMMARY.
(*Erase heading not required.*)

Hour, Date, Place	Summary of Events and Information	Remarks and References to Appendices
10.30 pm	One Section 9th Bty occupied Gun pits of one Section of 28th Bty position just S. of the RUE DU BOIS	
	3.7.15 G Turnbull Capt & Adjt for O.C. IV Bde RFA	

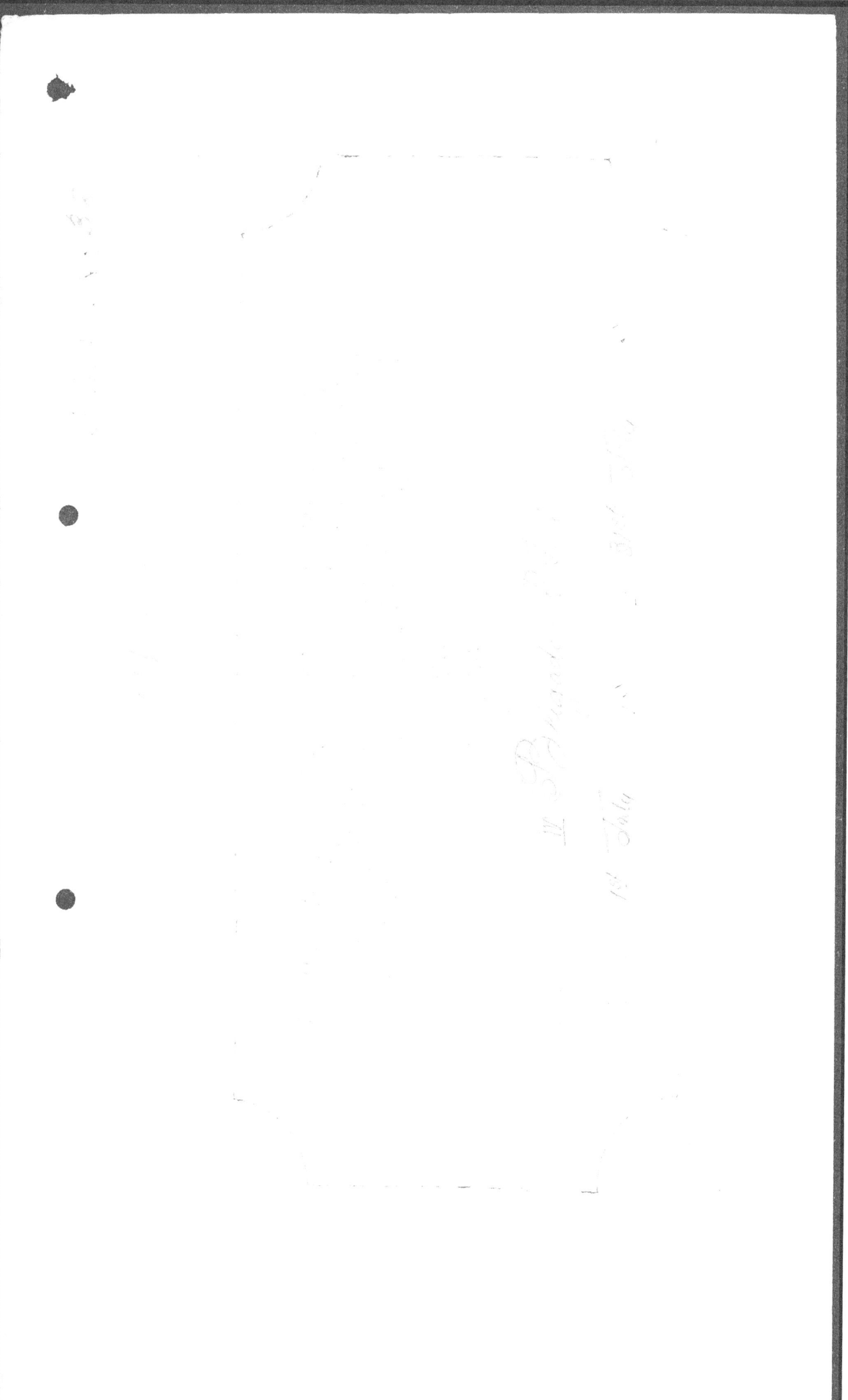

Army Form C. 2118.

Instructions regarding War Diaries and Intelligence Summaries are contained in F. S. Regs., Part II. and the Staff Manual respectively. Title pages will be prepared in manuscript.

WAR DIARY or INTELLIGENCE SUMMARY.

(Erase heading not required.)

IV Bde RFA — July 1915.

Hour, Date, Place		Summary of Events and Information	Remarks and References to Appendices
		A Misty morning –	Reference. Trench Map – VIOLAINES 1/10000.
1.7.15	1 am.	14th Bty fired on trench between Q11 + Q15 to impede working party – seen at dusk –	
	8 am.	Enemy's Howitzer shelled trenches near R5 doing slight dammage to parapet –	
	12.30 pm.	14th fired at trench near Q15 in Reply to Hostile guns shelling our trenches –	
	3.30 pm.	14th fired at reported Snipers –	
	3.30 to 4.30 pm.	Section of 7th Bty fired a few Rds for Registration – including Registration of Night lines –	
	5.55 pm	14th fired at Working party in trench near Q15 –	
	7.30 pm	66th fired 6 Rds at part of Fme COUR D'AVOINE at request of Infantry who reported having seen a periscope there –	
	10. pm.	Remaining two Sections of 7th Bty came into action – One man 66th Bty very slightly wounded today –	
2.7.15	5.20 am	14th Bty fired at working party at Q15 –	
–	12.15 pm	66th carried out further Registration –	
	~~[illegible]~~ 3.4 pm	66th fired 5 Rds on enemys trenches in Retaliation to 77mm Shelling 'B' Sub. trenches –	

(9 29 6) W 2794 100,000 8/14 H W V Forms/C. 2118/11.

Instructions regarding War Diaries and Intelligence Summaries are contained in F. S. Regs., Part II, and the Staff Manual respectively. Title pages will be prepared in manuscript.

WAR DIARY

or

INTELLIGENCE SUMMARY.

(Erase heading not required.)

Army Form C. 2118.

Hour, Date, Place	Summary of Events and Information	Remarks and References to Appendices

Army Form C. 2118.

Instructions regarding War Diaries and Intelligence Summaries are contained in F. S. Regs., Part II. and the Staff Manual respectively. Title pages will be prepared in manuscript.

WAR DIARY
or
INTELLIGENCE SUMMARY.
(Erase heading not required.)

Hour, Date, Place	Summary of Events and Information	Remarks and References to Appendices
4.7.15		
8.30 am	14th Bty fired a few Rds at Fme DU BOIS trenches in retaliation	
8.30 am	German aeroplane over left of 14th Bty – attacked by one of our planes + driven off –	
5.30 pm	14th fired a few Rds at Suspicious tree near Q20 in response to shelling of 'C' + 'D' Subsections –	
6.10 pm –	66th fired at Fme COUR D'AVOINE + Sandbagged house in retaliation to Germans shelling 'B' Subsection –	
7.45 pm	14th fired at party of Germans walking across open to fire trench near Q11 –	
	2Lieut E. JONES from 4th Bde A.C. to Hospital –	
5.7.15 –		
4 am to 5.45 am –	occasional Rds, 77 mm, falling on Support trenches between C + D Subsections from direction of LORGIES – 14th Bty	
5.25 am –	fired at Fme DU BOIS but did not check firing –	
	During the day 14th + 66th fired at German trenches in Retaliation	
6.5 pm	7th fired a few Rds at trench 100x S.W. of P14 at request of Infantry –	

(9 29 6) W 2794 100,000 8/14 H W V Forms/C. 2118/11.

Army Form C. 2118

Instructions regarding War Diaries and Intelligence Summaries are contained in F. S. Regs., Part II. and the Staff Manual respectively. Title pages will be prepared in manuscript.

WAR DIARY
or
INTELLIGENCE SUMMARY.

(Erase heading not required.)

Hour, Date, Place	Summary of Events and Information	Remarks and References to Appendices

W [illegible] 100,000 [illegible] H W V Forms/C. 2118/11.

Army Form C. 2118.

Instructions regarding War Diaries and Intelligence Summaries are contained in F. S. Regs., Part II. and the Staff Manual respectively. Title pages will be prepared in manuscript.

WAR DIARY
or
INTELLIGENCE SUMMARY.
(*Erase heading not required.*)

Hour, Date, Place	Summary of Events and Information	Remarks and References to Appendices
8.7.15 –		
3.45 + 4.30 a.m.	14th fired at working parties near Q15 + Q12 –	
6 a.m.	7th fired at request of Infantry on German trench S of P14.	
11 a.m.	66th Silenced Bomb gun near P13 which had been troublesome	
2.15 pm	IV Bde Hd Qrs shelled by 5.9 Howitzers – about 30 Rounds – all short except two – line plumb – one fell next dugout – A few Rds were fired in retaliation during the day –	
9.7.15 –	IV Bde Hd Qrs moved to new Quarters close to LA COUTURE Church.	
	LIEUT A.V. OLIVER-JONES accidentally wounded + sent to Hospital.	
	2/LIEUT T. WILKINS joined IV Bde + posted to IV Bde A.C.	
4.20 + 4.30 a.m –	7th + 66th fired on trench mortar near ~~[illegible]~~ P13 which was bombing our trenches –	
6.35 a.m	7th again fired on trench mortar in trenches S.W. of P14 –	
10.20 a.m	German aeroplane over 66th Bty but retreated on being fired at by our Anti-aircraft guns –	
4 p.m.	14th fired on Snipers in Fme DU BOIS –	
9 p.m. + 11 p.m.	66th fired salvoes on Q11 + Q12 where working parties were located last night —	

(9 29 6) W 2794 100,000 8/14 H W V Forms/C. 2118/11.

Instructions regarding War Diaries and Intelligence Summaries are contained in F. S. Regs., Part II. and the Staff Manual respectively. Title pages will be prepared in manuscript.

Army Form C. 2118.

WAR DIARY
or
INTELLIGENCE SUMMARY.

(Erase heading not required.)

Hour, Date, Place		Summary of Events and Information	Remarks and References to Appendices
10.7.15.			
		2/Lieut W. M. DRAKE joined IV Bde & posted to 14th Bty.	
	7.30 a.m.	14th fired on working party visible at Q15 - party dispersed	
	8.50 "	" " " " " " at of about 20 Germans at S22 a 5.5 - party ceased working & fled.	
		14th & 61st fired at intervals during the day at probable O.P's & German trenches in retaliation.	
11.7.15	12.30 a.m.	Relief of GARHWAL Bde by 21st Inf. Bde Completed.	
	11.25 a.m.	Enemy's heavy Howitzer shelled LA COUTURE.	
	3.50 p.m.	14th took part in Combined shoot with heavies on new structure near Q11 - structure completely demolished but only one "[illegible]" seen.	
		A few Rds were fired during the day in Retaliation.	
12.7.15	12.30 - 2 p.m.	14th Registered new from V2, V3, V6.	
	3 p.m.	66th fired 2 Rds at request of Inf. party at Fme COUR D'AVOINE as Snipers were v. active from there.	
		66th fired in Retaliation to Heavy Howitzers shelling our trenches	
11/12.		During the night 2 Sections 7th relieved 2 Sections 2nd Bty at M32 a 3.6.	

(9 29 6) W 2794 100,000 8/14 H W V Forms/C. 2118/11.

Army Form C. 2118.

Instructions regarding War Diaries and Intelligence Summaries are contained in F. S. Regs., Part II. and the Staff Manual respectively. Title pages will be prepared in manuscript.

WAR DIARY
or
INTELLIGENCE SUMMARY.
(*Erase heading not required.*)

Hour, Date, Place		Summary of Events and Information	Remarks and References to Appendices
12.7.15		7th Bty Registered new front with 2 Sections during the afternoon –	
	9.30 pm.	66th moved four guns to 8th Bty position M31 G98	
	10.45 "	Remaining Section of 7th relieved Section of 2nd Bty –	
13.7.15.	6.30 am	66th Carried out Registration on new front opposite ORCHARD POST.	
		During the day IV Bde Bty's took over liason with Inf. of 'E.F.G.' Subsections	
	10.45 am	German heavy Howitzer shelled left front of SNIPERS House – (7th O.P.).	
	5 pm	14th Registered further points in front of 'E' Subsection – a few Rounds were fired in retaliation at German trenches & distillery.	'E' Subsection – R. Welsh Fusiliers (14th)
	11.45 pm	Relief of BAREILLY Bde by 22nd Inf. Bde completed –	'F' " Warwickshire Regt. (66th)
14.7.15.	4.45 am.	14th fired on working party in Second line trench between V2 & V3. where considerable movement had been seen –	'G' " do. do. (7th)
		Enemy's 77 mm active during most of the day (at intervals)	
		Each Battery Carried out further Registration –	
	3.30 pm	14th dispersed working party about 100x S of the C in RICHEBOURG – S 10 d 8.5 –	

Instructions regarding War Diaries and Intelligence Summaries are contained in F. S. Regs., Part II. and the Staff Manual respectively. Title pages will be prepared in manuscript.

WAR DIARY
or
INTELLIGENCE SUMMARY.
(Erase heading not required.)

Army Form C. 2118.

Hour, Date, Place	Summary of Events and Information	Remarks and References to Appendices
15.7.15		
5.30 am	[illegible]	
7.15 am	[illegible]	
[illegible]	[illegible] 10.5 am [illegible]	
to 2.15 pm	[illegible]	
3.25 pm	[illegible]	
	[illegible] ESTAIRES [illegible]	
	[illegible]	
7.15 pm	[illegible]	
	2/Lieut D.F. FRASER rejoined [illegible]	
16.7.15	[illegible] W.B. D[illegible] [illegible]	
	[illegible] PRITCHARD [illegible]	
[illegible]	[illegible] (looked [illegible])	
12 noon	[illegible]	
to 2.15 pm	[illegible]	
5.25 pm	[illegible]	

9.29.6 W 2795 100,000 5/15 H W V Forms/C. 2118/11.

Army Form C. 2118.

Instructions regarding War Diaries and Intelligence Summaries are contained in F. S. Regs., Part II. and the Staff Manual respectively. Title pages will be prepared in manuscript.

WAR DIARY
or
INTELLIGENCE SUMMARY.
(Erase heading not required.)

Hour, Date, Place	Summary of Events and Information	Remarks and References to Appendices
17.7.15.	A quiet day — Nothing to Report —	
18.7.15. 10.am to 11.30 am	Enemy shelled SNIPERS HOUSE and Communicating trenches to RUE DU BOIS — Shoot commenced with field guns + continued with 15 Cm Howitzers — 4 Hits from latter on House and one on Inf. Hd. Quarters —	
12.30. pm	Field guns shelled fork RUE DU BERCEAUX - ALBERT ROAD.	
12.30 + 2.30 pm	14th Knocked out one loop hole just E of V3 —	
5. pm.	7th fired a few Rds in Retaliation (at request of Infantry) to German field guns shelling 'G' Subsection trenches —	
7.30 pm	14th fired on party of Germans carrying planks near V6 —	E Subsection — 1st S. STAFFORD. Regt. Bty 14th
7.35 pm	and on working party near R13 —	F. " 2nd QUEENS — 66th
11. pm.	Infantry of E. F. + G. Subsections relieved as per by Infantry as per margin —	G " do. 7th
19.7.15. 7.30 to 9 am.	German aeroplanes active on our front —	
8.25 a.m.	66th fired on working party near R13 —	
12.30 pm.	14th Registered Sally ports about 100x SW of V3 —	
2 pm + 5 pm.	14th " iron plates about 100x N of V3 —	
3.51 pm	14th fired 3 salvoes at R11 with aeroplane — aeroplane then broke down —	

(9 29 6) W 2794 100,000 8/14 H W V Forms/C. 2118/11.

Instructions regarding War Diaries and Intelligence Summaries are contained in F. S. Regs., Part II. and the Staff Manual respectively. Title pages will be prepared in manuscript.

WAR DIARY
or
INTELLIGENCE SUMMARY.
(Erase heading not required.)

Army Form C. 2118.

Hour, Date, Place	Summary of Events and Information	Remarks and References to Appendices
5.15 + 6.10 pm.	66th and 14th Registered front line German trench from V3 to V6 – our Infantry came out of fire trench during Registration as trenches very close together –	
20.7.15 6.40 am	14th fired at bomb gun about S10c6.5.	
6.40 + 7.50 am.	at Request of Infantry of 'B' Subsection, 7th Bty fired on German front trenches in Retaliation to Germans (77 mm) shelling our trenches – The 77 guns stopped firing at once –	
12.20 pm.	14th fired on German probable O.P. and trenches in Retaliation to 77 mm firing on our trenches –	
5.45 pm.	66th fired 12 Rds on German trenches in Retaliation for fire of trench mortar on our trenches and 77 mm which followed – Enemy stopped firing but Mortar not located –	
7 pm.	14th fired on Support lines in Retaliation to 77 mm firing at our trenches.	
7.45 pm.	14th fired at request of Infantry on trench mortar S10c7.8 – bombs coming from there –	
11.30 pm.	66th fired at working party at V6 – work ceased –	

(9 29 6) W 2794 100,000 8/14 H W V Forms/C. 2118/11.

Army Form C. 2118.

Instructions regarding War Diaries and Intelligence Summaries are contained in F. S. Regs., Part II. and the Staff Manual respectively. Title pages will be prepared in manuscript.

WAR DIARY
or
INTELLIGENCE SUMMARY.
(Erase heading not required.)

Hour, Date, Place	Summary of Events and Information	Remarks and References to Appendices
21.7.15		
5.30 am.	14th fired a few Rounds in Retaliation to 77mm shelling our trenches –	
12.40 pm.	14th + 66th fired on trenches V5 to V6 in retaliation to 77mm shelling our trenches	
2.30 pm.	14th fired at 77mm at M29 along with Canadian Heavy Bty –	
5.30 pm.	66th Registered R17E.	
	A few more Rds were fired in Retaliation –	
22.7.15. 9.30 am.	66th fired at enemys trenches at Request of Infantry whose Headquarters were being shelled by light Howitzer – Enemy did not stop so 48th Heavy asked to fire –	
9.40 am.	Enemy's Heavy Howitzer shelled SNIPERS House + Inf. Hd Quarters – 7th retaliated + 48th H. Battery Co-operated –	
11.45 am	14th fired at trenches at request from Infantry – 77mm shelling Support trenches	
12.25 pm	14th had three direct hits on O P at V7E – with H.E. – Good Rounds.	
5. + 5.30 pm	a few Rds were fired in Retaliation –	E Subsection BEDFORD'S 14th Bty
11.40 pm.	The 21st Inf. Bde. relieved the 22nd – Regiments as per margin –	F WILTSHIRE 66th –
23.7.15. 6.45 am	14th fired on two working parties 100x E of V2. parties dispersed –	G do. 7th –
8.27 am.	A few Heavy Howitzers (probably 15 cm) fell about 200x in front of 14th Bty direction LORGIES.	

(9 29 6) W 2794 100,000 8/14 H W V Forms/C. 2118/11.

Instructions regarding War Diaries and Intelligence Summaries are contained in F. S. Regs., Part II. and the Staff Manual respectively. Title pages will be prepared in manuscript.

WAR DIARY
or
INTELLIGENCE SUMMARY.
(Erase heading not required.)

Army Form C. 2118.

Hour, Date, Place	Summary of Events and Information	Remarks and References to Appendices

Instructions regarding War Diaries and Intelligence Summaries are contained in F. S. Regs., Part II. and the Staff Manual respectively. Title pages will be prepared in manuscript.

WAR DIARY
or
INTELLIGENCE SUMMARY.
(Erase heading not required.)

Army Form C. 2118.

Hour, Date, Place	Summary of Events and Information	Remarks and References to Appendices
12.40 pm.	Loud cheering was heard from the German trenches and a flag waved about –	
2.20 pm to 2.35 pm.	14th + 66th fired at probable O.P. + trenches in retaliation –	
3.30 pm.	14th Registered House R16.	
4.37 pm.	14th fired on V7E in Retaliation and stopped their fire –	
5.10 pm	66th Registered reported O.P. in NE corner Fme DU BOIS – One direct hit –	
6.45 pm to 7.15 pm.	15 shell fell close to IV Bde Hd Qrs. No damage done –	
8. pm.	7th fired at German trench in Retaliation –	
25.7.15 – 5. am.	66th fired 6 Rds at trenches near V3 in reply to 77 mm firing at our trenches – Enemy ceased firing –	
10.35 am.	14th fired at V7E and R17E in reply for 77 mm shelling E Subsection trenches – 77 mm stopped firing at once –	
	Three S.O.S. Test messages with firing were responded to during the morning	
	The 7th Bty have established a new O.P. – S10 b 39 – 'ROTUNDA'	
4.20 pm.	66th fired on trenches near V3 in reply to enemy shelling our Reserve trenches near LEICESTER LOUNGE – Enemy's fire ceased –	

Army Form C. 2118.

Instructions regarding War Diaries and Intelligence Summaries are contained in F. S. Regs., Part II. and the Staff Manual respectively. Title pages will be prepared in manuscript.

WAR DIARY
or
INTELLIGENCE SUMMARY.
(Erase heading not required.)

Hour, Date, Place		Summary of Events and Information	Remarks and References to Appendices
	4.45 pm.	14th dispersed working party near V.2.	
	6.50 pm.	66th fired on house near V7E where Huns were removing timber.	
	6.15 pm.	7th fired a few Rounds on suspected O.P. at V10 (West of Road) — Two hits on house & set it on fire.	
26.7.15	5. am.	14th got well into a large working party near R12 and dispersed them.	
	6.55 am.	11th fired at party hauling in wire near R11. and Regimental [illegible] between V5E and V6E.	
	10.45 am.	7th fired at party carrying planks and work going on near 65 - work ceased.	
	10.50 am.	12th fired 2 Salvoes at (working party) on parapet of trench 100x S of V.2. Party vanished.	
	11. am.	10th fired on Hun observer with glasses seen in 3rd line trench near V2 - 1 perfectly burst shell caused him to disappear in a cloud of dust.	
	6.45 pm.	11th fired at working party near V.6 — party dispersed —	
	do.	7th fired in Retaliation at request of Infantry.	
	5.35, 5.45 & 7.10 pm.	6 [illegible] were fired in Retaliation to Heavy Howitzer Shelling trenches and orchard —	

Army Form C. 2118.

Instructions regarding War Diaries and Intelligence Summaries are contained in F. S. Regs., Part II. and the Staff Manual respectively. Title pages will be prepared in manuscript.

WAR DIARY
or
INTELLIGENCE SUMMARY.
(*Erase heading not required.*)

Hour, Date, Place	Summary of Events and Information	Remarks and References to Appendices
7.30 pm.	7th Bty destroyed fly wheel SE of pt. 50 – This wheel has been in rapid motion all day but stopped after the 4th Round which nearly hit it – Large quantities of white wood splinters were thrown in the air on several occasions when shell fell near the wheel and one shell fell in some combustible or explosive as a dense cloud of grey smoke rose from the point which hung in the air for a considerable time –	
	The RITZ was hit during the afternoon & set on fire –	
27.7.15. 3.50 pm	14th fired at new loop hole in dug out 100x S.W. of V2 –	
6.50 pm	14th Registered an emplacement that looked likely to contain a M Gun in 2nd line behind V2.	
7.15 pm.	7th engaged new work which the Germans were constructing near pt 50. Several direct hits – The 8th Round of H.E. set fire to the work. The fire spread over a front of 25x – The flames attained the height of 15 feet & gave off a dense black smoke which seems to indicate burning oil, which in turn seems to have set fire to the wood used for revetting purposes – The fire did not die down till 10.15 pm.	

(9 29 6) W 2794 100,000 8/14 H W V Forms/C. 2118/11.

Instructions regarding War Diaries and Intelligence Summaries are contained in F. S. Regs., Part II. and the Staff Manual respectively. Title pages will be prepared in manuscript.

WAR DIARY
or
INTELLIGENCE SUMMARY.
(Erase heading not required.)

Army Form C. 2118.

Hour, Date, Place	Summary of Events and Information	Remarks and References to Appendices

Instructions regarding War Diaries and Intelligence Summaries are contained in F. S. Regs., Part II. and the Staff Manual respectively. Title pages will be prepared in manuscript.

WAR DIARY
or
INTELLIGENCE SUMMARY.
(*Erase heading not required.*)

Army Form C. 2118.

Hour, Date, Place		Summary of Events and Information	Remarks and References to Appendices
	6.40 pm	7th Bty registered machine gun emplacement S11 a 0.4 – There appears to be two emplacements there about 20x apart from each other – Right one concealed by filled Sand bags hung in front of it –	
	9.45 pm	14th fired 4 Rds at S16 b 5.0, where large working party had been seen at daylight.	
30.7.15.	7.30 to 9.30 am	Enemy's Heavy Howitzer shelled 7th O.P. – The 48th Heavy Bty retaliated by engaging enemy's Bty at T9 A 5.5. and Fme DU BIEZ – (O.P.)	
	4.15 pm	14th fired a Series at obvious O.P. about 23 d 8.6 – House with loopholes on side face.	
	6.10 pm	66th Registered (I) Sally ports near S10 c 6.3. (II) – Fort near S16 a 8.4 – (III) + end of trench at S16 b 1.6.	
	7.30 pm	66th fired on machine gun emplacement at S10 c 2.1 as the M.G. had fired a few Rounds from there a short time previously –	
31.7.15.	8.45 am	Hostile aeroplane over RICHEBOURG – Engaged by 'Archie' – retired E –	
	3. pm	14th Co-operated with 31st How. Bty on House (O.P.) at S23 d 8.5	
	4. pm	14th fired on working party at S10 d 3.7 –	
	7.35 pm.	14th fired at two men looking over parapet & claim to have bagged both –	

2.8.15.

[illegible] Capt
Adj IV Bde RFA

(9 29 6) W 2794 100,000 8/14 H W V Forms/C. 2118/11.

Serial No. 38

121/6958

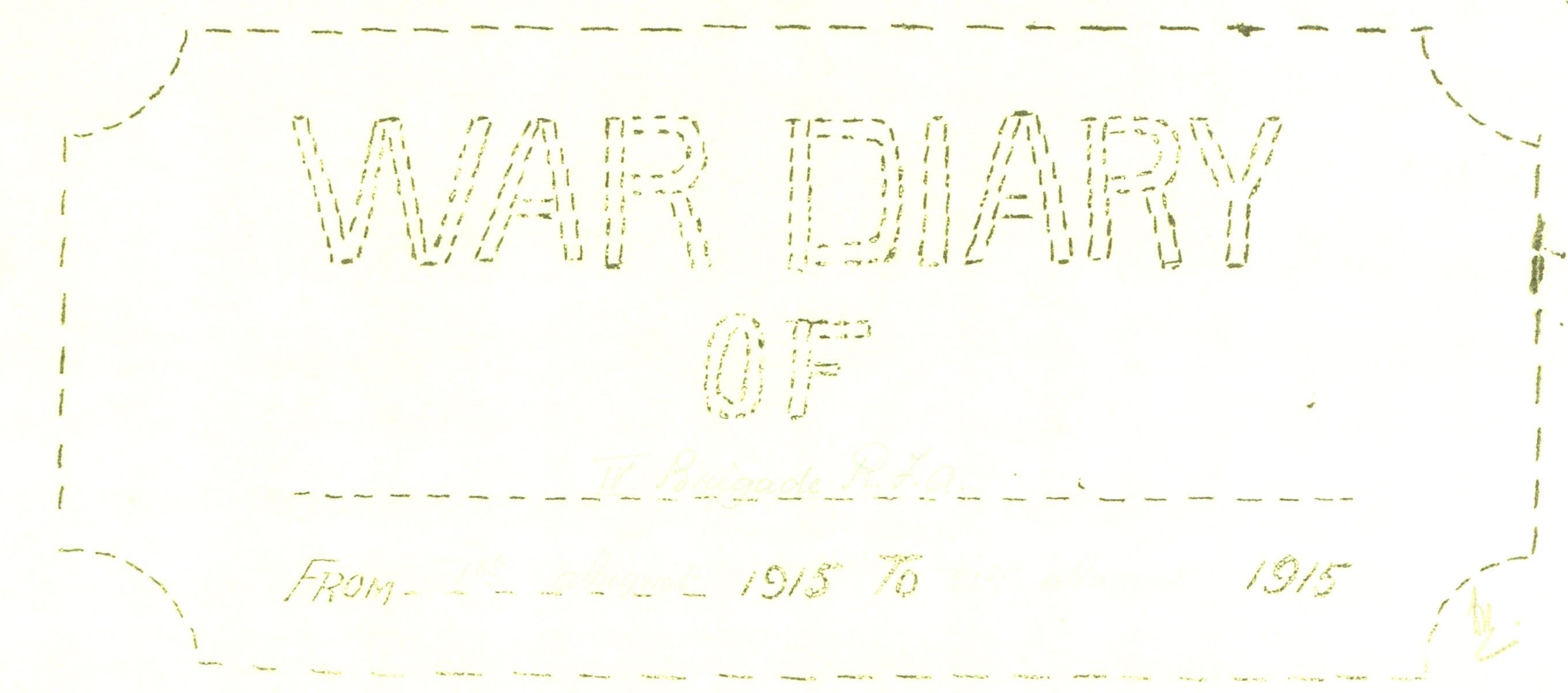

WAR DIARY

OF

IV Brigade R.F.A.

FROM 1st August 1915 To [illegible] 1915

Army Form C. 2118.

Instructions regarding War Diaries and Intelligence Summaries are contained in F. S. Regs., Part II. and the Staff Manual respectively. Title pages will be prepared in manuscript.

WAR DIARY
or
INTELLIGENCE SUMMARY.
(*Erase heading not required.*)

IV Bde RFA
August –

Hour, Date, Place	Summary of Events and Information	Remarks and References to Appendices
1.8.15		
6.34 am.	14th fired at Small working party behind V2, in latrine, Two men seen to fall –	
8.10 am	" " " Working party in vicinity of V2 – party dispersed –	
8.40 to 9.40 am.	Three Heavy Howitzer shell fell in 7th Bty position – No damage done – about 30 others fell about 300x behind Bty position –	
9.55 am.	66th fired 3 Section Salvoes at party working on parapet of front trench at S10C64 – party disappeared –	
11.16 am.	14th fired at German trenches in Retaliation to German 77mm shelling our trenches.	
1.45 pm	" " a few Rds at O.P. – House S23b17 – one direct hit –	
6.45 pm.	77mm shelled RUE DU BOIS close to 14th & 66th OPs – Both Batteries retaliated on German trenches & O.P. at S17b18 – 77mm retaliated by violently shelling RICHEBOURG –	Right Subsection. 1st H.L.I. 14th Bty.
2.8.15 3.58 am	14th fired at bomb thrower near S10C31.	Centre " 15th SIKHS + 2Coo 1/4 GR 66th + 7th Btys
	During the night of 1/2 August the SIRHIND Bde relieved the 21st Inf. Bde	
	The base plug of an A.P. Shell fired yesterday close to 7th Bty 2nd O.P. measured approximately 9" – The shell would therefore appear to be at least a 28 cm. – The shell had a steel pointed nose –	Left " 4th Kings – 84th Bty – 84th Bty under OC IV Bde to cover SIRHIND Bde front –

(9 29 6) W 2794 100,000 8/14 H W V Forms/C. 2118/11.

Instructions regarding War Diaries and Intelligence Summaries are contained in F. S. Regs., Part II. and the Staff Manual respectively. Title pages will be prepared in manuscript.

WAR DIARY
or
INTELLIGENCE SUMMARY.
(Erase heading not required.)

Army Form C. 2118.

Hour, Date, Place		Summary of Events and Information	Remarks and References to Appendices
	5.25 am.	77 mm shelled Support + Communication trenches of Right Subsection – 14th Retaliated on German trenches – 77 mm stopped –	
	5.45 am.	77 mm shelled 14th + 66th OPs – Both Batteries retaliated at front + Support trenches + 77 mm stopped at once –	
		Remainder of day very quiet –	
2/3.8.15		A very quiet morning –	
	4.10 pm.	86th Bty dispersed a working party near S11a 23 –	
	10.30 & 11.30 pm.	Two Sections 59th Bty relieved two Sections 14th Bty – Sections of 14th to W. line	
		" " 93rd " " " " " 7th Bty.	
		" " 7th " went into new position at M21b64.	
3/4.8.15	about 11 pm.	One Section 59th Bty relieved remaining Section 14th Bty – 14th Sect. to Wagon line.	
		" " 94th " " one " 66th – 66th " " " "	
		" " 93rd " " remaining " 7th Bty	
		" 7th went into action at M21b64.	
4.8.15	10.00 am.	183 Bde took over SIRHIND Bde front. IV Bde RFA (less 7th Bty) came back to rest – Bde HQrs to LES AMUSOIRES 14th + 66th west end of ST FLORIS – 7th Bty came under OC XIII Bde RFA.	
	11 pm.	Remaining 2 Sections 66th Bty were relieved by 2 Sections 94th Bty –	

(B 29 6) W 2794 100,000 8/14 H W V Forms/C. 2118/11.

Army Form C. 2118.

Instructions regarding War Diaries and Intelligence Summaries are contained in F. S. Regs., Part II. and the Staff Manual respectively. Title pages will be prepared in manuscript.

WAR DIARY
or
INTELLIGENCE SUMMARY.
(Erase heading not required.)

Hour, Date, Place	Summary of Events and Information	Remarks and References to Appendices
	LIEUT D.A.S BECK A.V.C left Bde & posted 2nd DIVISION –	
5.8.15	2Lieut C.B.T. PARCELL rejoined 14th Bty – He had been away about 3 months in charge of bomb guns –	
	Btys overhauling & painting guns –	
6.8.15.	The Col & Adj reconnoitred about 20 positions 'BOUT DEVILLE System'	
~~[illegible]~~ – 30.7.15.	2LIEUTS. P.T. WHEELER, & R.M. DAVIES joined Bde – former posted to 14th Bty – latter to 7th Bty –	
7.8.15 –	Rest.	
8.8.15	Hd Qrs – 14th Bty – 66th Bty, and Column changed billets to about 3 Miles N.W. of MERVILLE –	
~~7~~ 11.8.15 –	14th Bty went into action under O.C. IX Bde R.F.A.	
12.8.15.	Lieut G BARRY A.V.C. (Temp. Com.) joined the Bde –	
13.8.15.	2Lieut D.R. CHRISTIE (Special Reserve) joined the Bde. posted to 66th Bty.	
15.8.15.	Lieut R.B. BATES from 66th Bty to D.A.C MEERUT DIV –	
	2Lieut A. SHATTOCK attached to 7th Bty –	
17.8.15.	Lieut W.H.C. METCALFE attached to 14th from C 87th Bty –	
18.8.15.	B.S.M. Stancombe left 7th Bty having received commission as 2Lieut & proceeded to England –	

(9 29 6) W 2794 100,000 8/14 H W V Forms/C. 2118/11.

Instructions regarding War Diaries and Intelligence Summaries are contained in F. S. Regs., Part II. and the Staff Manual respectively. Title pages will be prepared in manuscript.

WAR DIARY
or
INTELLIGENCE SUMMARY.
(Erase heading not required.)

Army Form C. 2118.

Hour, Date, Place		Summary of Events and Information	Remarks and References to Appendices
19.8.15.		2nd Lieut A. SHATTOCK, attached 7th Bty, rejoined his Unit – 87 Bde R.F.A.	
21.8.15.		Lieut W. H. C. METCALFE, attached 14th Bty, rejoined his Unit – C 87 Bty R.F.A.	
26.8.15.		Sgt LOWCOCK. A. ~~as~~ left 14th Bty R.F.A. having received Commission as 2nd LIEUT – date of Commission 10.8.15 –	
26.8.15 –	9 pm.	Two Sections 66th Bty from Rest went into action at M33 a.6.	Map, Sheet 36 SW 1/20000.
27.8.15 –	9 pm	One Section " " " " " " " " "	
		66th Battery under O.C. XI Bde R.F.A.	
27.8.15.	9 pm.	IV Bde RFA Amn Column from rest went to new billets R10a 37.	36 A S E.
	"	One Section 14th Bty came out of action & went into action at M6a 87 and relieved one section 85th Bty. 66th Bty relieved 83rd Bty.	
	"	One Section 7th Bty came out of action & went into action at M2b69 and relieved one Section 84th Bty. 7th & 14th Sections under XI Bde RFA.	
28.8.15	10pm.	One Section 7th & 14th Btys relieved one Section 84th & 85th Btys –	
during Night 26/27 and 27/28.		GARHWAL Bde relieved ~~[illegible]~~ ~~[illegible]~~ by 60th Inf. Bde –	
during night 28/29.		GARHWAL Bde took over front of IND IV.	

(9 29 6) W 2791 100,000 8/14 H W V Forms/C. 2118/11.

Instructions regarding War Diaries and Intelligence Summaries are contained in F. S. Regs., Part II. and the Staff Manual respectively. Title pages will be prepared in manuscript.

WAR DIARY
or
INTELLIGENCE SUMMARY.
(Erase heading not required.)

Army Form C. 2118.

Hour, Date, Place		Summary of Events and Information	Remarks and References to Appendices
29.8.15.	9 pm	Remaining Sections of 7th + 14th relieved Sections of 84th + 86th –	
30.8.15.	10 am	OC. IV Bde took over front IND IV from O.C. 11th Bde RFA	
		C89 Howitzer also under O.C. IV Bde RFA.	
	2.50 pm	14th fired four Rounds – Registration –	
	5.30 pm	7th – 16 " " –	
	6. pm	66th – 13 " in Conjunction with 9.2" – at supposed gas apparatus –	
		Capt + Adj P. TURNBULL promoted Major – 2nd Gazette of today –	
31.8.15.		a few Rounds were fired to Register certain points of enemy's trench –	
	2.20 pm	66th fired 2 Rds at working party S56 76.	
	4.40 + 4.50 pm	14th + 66th fired at working party at S5663 + S5676	

1.9.15

P Turnbull Major
Adj IV Bde RFA

Serial No. 38.

121/7286

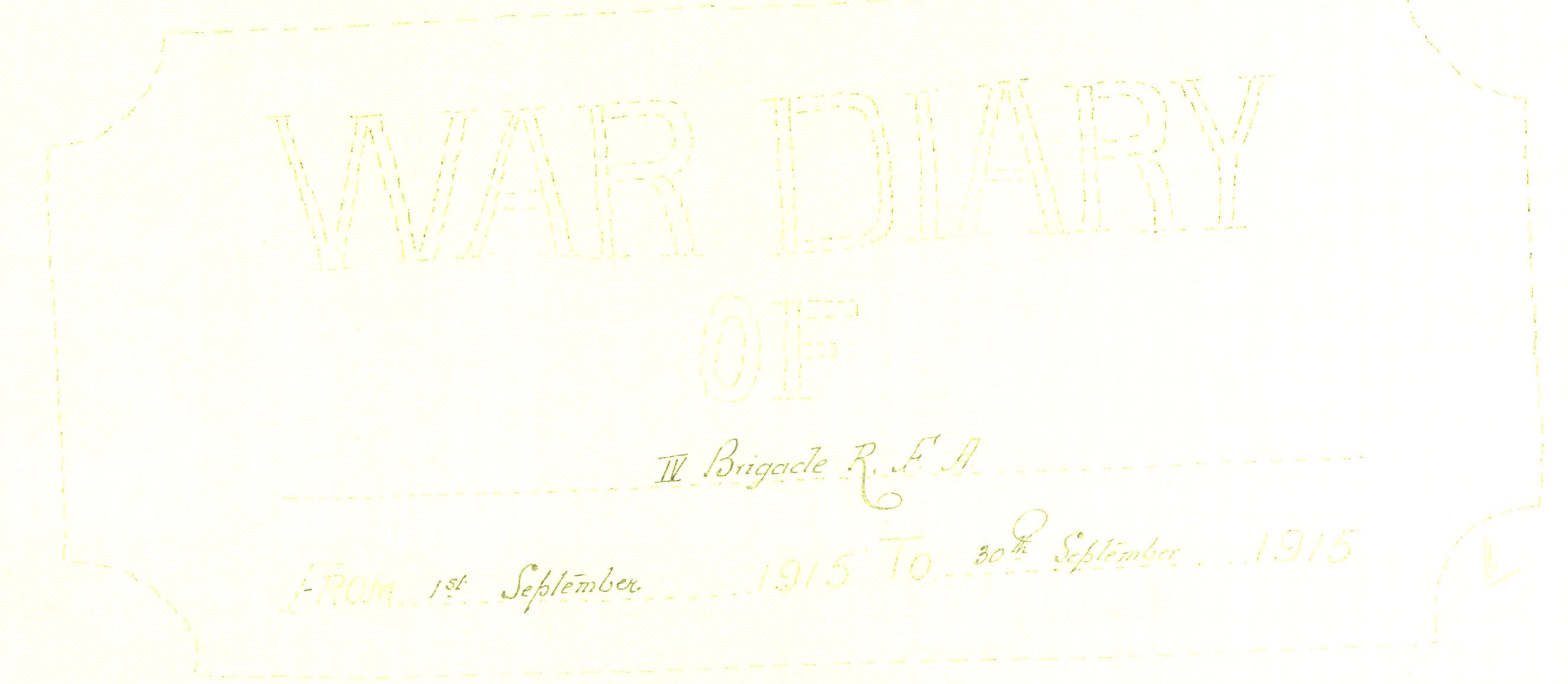

WAR DIARY

OF

IV Brigade R.F.A.

FROM 1st September 1915 TO 30th September 1915

Instructions regarding War Diaries and Intelligence Summaries are contained in F. S. Regs., Part II. and the Staff Manual respectively. Title pages will be prepared in manuscript.

WAR DIARY
or
INTELLIGENCE SUMMARY. IV Bde RFA.

(Erase heading not required.)

Army Form C. 2118.

Hour, Date, Place	Summary of Events and Information	Remarks and References to Appendices
1.9.15.		
5.30am	66th fired at Huns entering House at S6a75. At least 5 Hit.	Trench Map
4. pm	" " " trees behind S6a65 in conjunction with C89	36 S.W.
	How. Bty who fired at trench just in front of trees. How Bty	
	did good work as several explosions were heard. The	
	explosions continued for at least an hour.	
4.30 & 4.45pm	7th & 14th fired a few Rds in retaliation to 77 mm shelling	Right Subsection
	our trenches.	59th Rifles 7th Bty
During Night 1/2.	JULLUNDUR Bde relieved GHARWAL Bde	47th Sikhs 14th "
2.9.15. 2 pm	66th fired four Rds at trench S5b78. Large party of Germans seen	Left Subsection 1st Manchesters 66 "
	to pass carrying timber. dropped two of them.	
	A few Rounds were fired during the day for Registration	
3.45 to 4.30pm	About 15 77 mm. fell on our fire & reserve trenches.	
5.10 to 5.40pm	German aeroplane flying East & West SE of NEUVE CHAPELLE	
	apparently observing fire for Heavy Bty.	
During Night 2/3.	2 Sections 7th were relieved by 2 Sections 84th Bty	
	1 " 14 was " " 1 " 85th "	
	2 " 66th were " " 2 " 83rd "	

Instructions regarding War Diaries and Intelligence Summaries are contained in F. S. Regs., Part II, and the Staff Manual respectively. Title pages will be prepared in manuscript.

WAR DIARY
or
INTELLIGENCE SUMMARY.
(Erase heading not required.)

IV Bde. R.F.A.

Army Form C. 2118.

Hour, Date, Place	Summary of Events and Information	Remarks and References to Appendices
Night 2/3	2 Sections 7th went into action at M 21 b 75 relieving 2 Sections 26th Bty.	
	1 " 11th " " " " M 21 a 62 " 1 Section 2nd Bty.	
	2 " 66th " to Wagon line.	
2.9.15	10 p.m. O.C. XI Bde. Batteries took over Command from O.C. IV Bde. R.F.A.	
	66th started to dig new position at M 28 c central.	
Night 2/3	Remaining Sections of 7th & 11th relieved Sections of 26th & 2nd Btys.	
	Section of 66th to Wagon line, on relief by XI Bde. Batteries.	
4.9.15	4 p.m. O.C. XI Bde. R.F.A. took over [illegible] from O.C. IV Bde. R.F.A.	
	12 noon 77 mm [illegible] shelled communication trenches and [illegible]	
	12 noon 11th registered enemy's support trenches.	
	1 p.m. 77 mm + 15 cm shelled farm M 22 b 10.1, 6 rounds each.	
	1.50 p.m. 15 cm from direction of AUBERS shelled [illegible] road at M 22 c 25	
	[illegible] fired 2 rounds [illegible] M 26 a 77 for identification purposes.	
	5 p.m. [illegible] registered enemy's fire trench [illegible] of [illegible]	
	8.15 & 8.50 p.m. [illegible] fired on enemy's fire trench [illegible] [illegible]	
	night lines.	

9 29 6 W 2751 100,000 5/14 H W V Forms/C. 2118/11.

Instructions regarding War Diaries and Intelligence Summaries are contained in F. S. Regs., Part II. and the Staff Manual respectively. Title pages will be prepared in manuscript.

WAR DIARY or INTELLIGENCE SUMMARY.

(*Erase heading not required.*)

IV Bde. R.F.A.

Army Form C. 2118.

Hour, Date, Place		Summary of Events and Information	Remarks and References to Appendices
Night 4/5		DEHRA DUN Bde. relieved BAREILLY Bde. on front line of Section IND. 5.	
5·9·15	12·35 a.m	On completion of reliefs O.C. IV Bde. R.F.A. took over command of the artillery in support of IND. 5. "A" sub-section.	7th on right } 14th on left } 4th Seaforths.
	8·4 a.m.	77 mm shelled our support trenches behind the MOATED GRANGE.	
	2·15 p.m.	10·5 c.m. from direction of AUBERS shelled SIGN POST LANE (5 rounds)	
	3·00 p.m	77 mm " " BAS POMMEREAU fired 6 rounds on above road.	
	3·20 p.m.	A few 77 mm shells fell near Cross Road at M 22 c 35.	
	5·0 p.m.	7th registered & shelled possible enemy's O.P. in BRICK HEAP at S 6 a 75	
5·9·15		Maj. & Adj. E. Turnbull (P. TURNBULL) to 17th Division	
		Lt. J. F. HOTCHESSON from MEERUT D.A.C. attached to 7th Bty.	
6·9·15	9·30 – 11 a.m	10·5 c.m. from direction of BAS POMMEREAU fired occasional shells at vicinity of M 22 central	
	10·50 a.m	77 mm shelled a working party in front of MOULIN farm, 8 rounds but no casualties.	
	2·40 p.m	14th fired 7 rounds at new small emplacement in fire trench at M 36 a 49	

(9 29 6) W 2794 100,000 8/14 H W V Forms/C. 2118/11.

Instructions regarding War Diaries and Intelligence Summaries are contained in F. S. Regs., Part II. and the Staff Manual respectively. Title pages will be prepared in manuscript.

WAR DIARY
or
INTELLIGENCE SUMMARY.
(Erase heading not required.)

IV Bde. R.F.A.

Army Form C. 2118.

Hour, Date, Place		Summary of Events and Information	Remarks and References to Appendices
6.9.15	11.15 p.m.	2nd fired 2 rounds on M.G. loop-hole in fire trench opposite the DUCKS BILL where movement had been noticed. 4th also fired [illegible] four rounds on German trenches for [illegible] and [illegible] during the [illegible].	
	5.15 p.m.	7th fired 2 rounds in [illegible] of [illegible] [illegible].	
7.9.15	5.20 p.m.	7th [illegible] support trenches of [illegible] [illegible] with 6 rounds.	
	8.45 p.m.	15 p.m. [illegible] of [illegible] POMMEREAU dropped 12 shells in vicinity of [illegible] BARBEE and [illegible] in M 26 a. [illegible] German [illegible] [illegible], [illegible] fire on [illegible] [illegible] [illegible] [illegible] [illegible] 9 p.m.	
	4.30 p.m.	[illegible] German [illegible] dropped a coloured paper balloon ([illegible] 22 [illegible]) which fell at M 25 c 14, it is [illegible] [illegible] [illegible] [illegible]	

[illegible]

W 2794 [illegible] Forms C. 2118 II.

Army Form C. 2118.

Instructions regarding War Diaries and Intelligence Summaries are contained in F. S. Regs., Part II. and the Staff Manual respectively. Title pages will be prepared in manuscript.

WAR DIARY
or
INTELLIGENCE SUMMARY.
(*Erase heading not required.*)

IV Bde. R.F.A.

Hour, Date, Place		Summary of Events and Information	Remarks and References to Appendices
	2·50 p.m.	10·5 c.m. fired 20 shells on trenches of IND 5"B" from BAS POMMEREAU.	
7·9·15	3·30 p.m.	7th Registered house in S 6 a 9585.	
	4·30 p.m	14th " fired 4 rounds in verification of Zero and Night lines.	
	During day	A/61 registered S 6 a 53, S 6 a 98 & S 6 a 56.	
	"	B/61 " MIN DU PIETRE & farm at T 2 b 16.	
		Col. L.A.C. GORDON. C.B. left Bde. on appointment to C.R.A. of MEERUT Div.	
		Maj. W.P. PAYNTER of 14th Bty. took over duties of acting Colonel.	
		2/Lieut P.T. WHEELER from 14th Bty to Bde. H.Q. Staff taking over duties of Orderly Officer vice 2/Lieut C.C. MIMS acting Adjutant.	
8·9·15	1·15 p.m.	10·5 c.m. gun from direction of BAS POMMEREAU shelled trenches near the SUNKEN ROAD and 14th retaliated on house at M 36 b 84.	
	2·30 p.m.	14th registered house at M 36 a 54 with 6 rounds.	
	4·10 p.m	14th silenced with one round a machine-gun firing on our aeroplane.	
	4·15 p.m.	7th registered houses at M 36 c 0035 and T 1 b 79 firing 18 rounds.	
	6·45 p.m.	14th fired 2 rounds to verify line on trench at M 36 c 87.	
	10·5 p.m.	Relief of 4th Seaforths by 2nd Gurkhas in IND 5 "A" sub-section completed.	

(9 29 6) W 2794 100,000 8/14 H W V Forms/C. 2118/11.

Army Form C. 2118.

Instructions regarding War Diaries and Intelligence Summaries are contained in F. S. Regs., Part II. and the Staff Manual respectively. Title pages will be prepared in manuscript.

WAR DIARY
or
INTELLIGENCE SUMMARY.
(Erase heading not required.)

IV Bde R.F.A.

Hour, Date, Place	Summary of Events and Information	Remarks and References to Appendices
8.9.15	2/Lieut. F. M. SHEPHERD (Special Res.) joined from 1st Reserve Bde. R.F.A. and was posted to IV Bde. R.F.A. Ammunition Column.	
[illegible]	7/61 registered [illegible] 6 p 2 8 [illegible] B 2 [illegible] p 56	
	3/61 registered and [illegible] [illegible] X 21 [illegible] T 2 p 10.	
9.9.15 2.15 p.m.	[illegible] [illegible] at M 2 d [illegible]	
5.50 [illegible]	7th [illegible] at S 6 p [illegible] M 26 c 00 [illegible]	
	[illegible]	
[illegible]	10th [illegible]	
	[illegible]	
	[illegible] at M [illegible]	
	[illegible] position [illegible]	
	[illegible]	
During [illegible]	[illegible] continued [illegible]	
	77 [illegible] position of LA RUSSIE [illegible]	
	[illegible] GRANGE [illegible] [illegible]	
	[illegible]	

Instructions regarding War Diaries and Intelligence Summaries are contained in F. S. Regs., Part II. and the Staff Manual respectively. Title pages will be prepared in manuscript.

WAR DIARY
or
INTELLIGENCE SUMMARY. IV Bde. R.F.A.

(Erase heading not required.)

Army Form C. 2118.

Hour, Date, Place		Summary of Events and Information	Remarks and References to Appendices
9.9.15	9.10 p.m.	14th fired 8 rounds on PIETRE Cross Roads at the request of Infantry who reported hearing transport moving there.	
	10.50 "	Section of B/76th Bde. R.F.A. came into action for instruction and practice under O.C. 7th, relieving section of 7th. Section 7th to wagon lines.	
10.9.15	10.10 a.m.	77 mm from direction of LA ROSSIE ~~fired~~ 4 shells at the MOATED GRANGE.	
	4.00 p.m.	Our antiaircraft guns brought down a German aviatik flying over their lines This biplane fell about ½ mile behind the German lines on low ground which made identification very difficult. 7th could see part of one wing above the trees apparently about S 6 b 45 & fired a number of shrapnel & H.E. at the wreck. 7th also fired several salvos during the night at parties attempting to remove it. A/61st & several other Howitzer and Field Batteries also opened fire.	
	5.10 p.m.	14th fired a few rounds to silence a machine-gun firing on our aeroplane.	
	During day	A/61st fired on an observing party & B/61st continued registration.	
	" "	B/76th fired 37 rounds for registration & instruction.	

Army Form C. 2118.

Instructions regarding War Diaries and Intelligence Summaries are contained in F. S. Regs., Part II, and the Staff Manual respectively. Title pages will be prepared in manuscript.

WAR DIARY
or
INTELLIGENCE SUMMARY. IV Bde. R.F.A.

(Erase heading not required.)

Hour, Date, Place	Summary of Events and Information	Remarks and References to Appendices
10.9.15	Major S. F. STALLARD from [illegible] R.F.A. [illegible] assumed command of IV Bde. R.F.A.	
	Capt. [illegible] PAYNTER [illegible]	
[illegible]	[illegible]	
	[illegible]	
	[illegible]	
	[illegible]	
[illegible]	[illegible]	
[illegible]	[illegible]	

[illegible]

Instructions regarding War Diaries and Intelligence Summaries are contained in F. S. Regs., Part II. and the Staff Manual respectively. Title pages will be prepared in manuscript.

WAR DIARY
or
INTELLIGENCE SUMMARY. IV Bde. R.F.A.
(Erase heading not required.)

Army Form C. 2118.

Hour, Date, Place		Summary of Events and Information	Remarks and References to Appendices
12.9.15	2.40 p.m	77 mm fired about 12 shells on front line trench of IND. 5. "A" subsection 60th How. Bty. were asked to retaliate which they immediately did.	
	4.40	114th fired several rounds on the concrete emplacement in M 30 c.	
	5.00	B/76th fired on suspected position of "Minenwerfer" also on row of brushwood suspected of being cover for working party.	
	5.30 – 6	114th fired on working party in M 36 a 4.8	
During night	12/13	GARHWAL and BAREILLY Bdes. relieved DEHRA DUN Bde on front line of IND. 5. Section ("A" and "B" sub-sections respectively).	
	10.00	Infantry reliefs in "A" sub-section completed, 39th GARHWAL RIFLES and 1/3rd LONDONS relieving 2nd GURKHAS	on right 7th Bty. on left 114th Bty.
13.9.15	9.00 a.m.	10.5 c.m. Howitzer searched N. end of RUGBY ROAD with about 30 shells.	
	1.45 p.m	A/61st & B/61st continued practice, scoring several direct hits on houses.	
	3.20	114th fired a few rounds on house where M.G. emplacement was reported & on road nearby M 36 a 4.4.	
	3.30	B/76 registered house at S 6 c 1.8 and brick heap at S 6 a 7.5	
	5.30	15 c.m. fired 8 rounds on house at M 35 d 1.8	

Army Form C. 2118.

Instructions regarding War Diaries and Intelligence Summaries are contained in F. S. Regs., Part II. and the Staff Manual respectively. Title pages will be prepared in manuscript.

WAR DIARY
or
INTELLIGENCE SUMMARY.
(*Erase heading not required.*)

Hour, Date, Place	Summary of Events and Information	Remarks and References to Appendices

W 7251 ... H.W.V. Forms/C. 2118/11.

Army Form C. 2118.

Instructions regarding War Diaries and Intelligence Summaries are contained in F. S. Regs., Part II. and the Staff Manual respectively. Title pages will be prepared in manuscript.

WAR DIARY or INTELLIGENCE SUMMARY. IV Bde. R.F.A.

(Erase heading not required.)

Hour, Date, Place		Summary of Events and Information	Remarks and References to Appendices
14·9·15		pump since a cloud of steam was seen to rise & the pump stopped.	
	5·20 p.m.	14th registered houses at N 21 d 9·1 M36 d 88 and M36 b 10·3.	
	8·55	14th fired a few rounds on enemy's fire trench in retaliation.	
15·9·15	8·25 a.m.	77 mm from direction of LA RUSSIE shelled with a few rounds tram-rail-head near SUNKEN ROAD communication trench.	
	8·50	The same battery searched along tram-way near support trenches.	
	11·10	14th registered various points in front of DUCK'S BILL.	
	12 noon	14th fired six rounds on fire trench to stop rifle & M.G. fire on one of our aeroplanes.	
	2-30 p.m.	7th fired 104 rounds continuing the test of A.X. with 100 fuze.	
	4·00	A/108 registered houses in vicinity of M 36 a 77, and wood in T1 b also AUBERS CHURCH.	
	4·15	77 mm from direction of HT. POMMEREAU fired 15 shells in vicinity of M 29 a.	
	5·30	14th fired a few rounds in retaliation to 77 mm shelling SUNKEN ROAD.	

(9 29 6) W 2794 100,000 8/14 H W V Forms/C. 2118/11.

Instructions regarding War Diaries and Intelligence Summaries are contained in F. S. Regs., Part II. and the Staff Manual respectively. Title pages will be prepared in manuscript.

WAR DIARY
or
INTELLIGENCE SUMMARY.
(Erase heading not required.)

Army Form C. 2118.

Hour, Date, Place	Summary of Events and Information	Remarks and References to Appendices

W 594 100,000 8/14 H W V Forms/C. 2118/11.

Army Form C. 2118.

Instructions regarding War Diaries and Intelligence Summaries are contained in F. S. Regs., Part II. and the Staff Manual respectively. Title pages will be prepared in manuscript.

WAR DIARY
or
INTELLIGENCE SUMMARY. IV Bde. R.F.A.

(*Erase heading not required.*)

Hour, Date, Place	Summary of Events and Information	Remarks and References to Appendices
17·9·15 During afternoon	14th registered four houses in vicinity of M 36 d —	
11.15 p.m.	A field-gun from direction of BAS POMMEREAU fired 5 shells, apparently at 14th Bty position, which fell about 250x short. They had a very flat trajectory & broke up into minute pieces, bursting just after graze; no fuzes were found.	
12 noon	10.5 cm from Ht POMMEREAU fired 10 rounds in vicinity of tram line near EBENEZER FARM.	
8.00 p.m.	Section of A/108 withdrawn & replaced by section of 14th.	
18·9·15 11.20 a.m.	77 mm shelled our support trenches & 14th promptly retaliated on enemy's fire trench.	
2.35 p.m.	7th registered houses at M 36 d 2.5.	
4.30 -	77 mm from BAS POMMEREAU was again active on our trenches so 7th retaliated on Night lines.	
During day	It was noticed that German aeroplanes were more active.	
9.45 p.m.	Relief of GARHWAL Bde by DEHRA DUN Bde was completed in IND 5 "A" sub-section.	4th Seaforths - 14th Bty left. 2/2nd Gurkhas - 7th " right.

(9 29 6) W 2794 100,000 8/14 H W V Forms/C. 2118/11.

Instructions regarding War Diaries and Intelligence Summaries are contained in F. S. Regs., Part II. and the Staff Manual respectively. Title pages will be prepared in manuscript.

WAR DIARY

or

INTELLIGENCE SUMMARY.

(Erase heading not required.)

Army Form C. 2118.

Hour, Date, Place	Summary of Events and Information	Remarks and References to Appendices
[illegible]	[illegible]	
[illegible]	[illegible]	
10.00 p.m.	[illegible]	

W 2594 ... Forms/C. 2118/11.

Army Form C. 2118.

Instructions regarding War Diaries and Intelligence Summaries are contained in F. S. Regs., Part II. and the Staff Manual respectively. Title pages will be prepared in manuscript.

WAR DIARY
or
INTELLIGENCE SUMMARY. IV Bde. R.F.A.
(*Erase heading not required.*)

Hour, Date, Place		Summary of Events and Information	Remarks and References to Appendices
21.9.15	8.00 p.m.	7th carried out their allotted tasks, in addition to maintaining the responsibility for their portion of front, shelling likely O.Ps. and defended houses. Also shelling probable M.G. emplacements, a number of selected points and a steady fire on PIETRE Cross-roads & vicinity.	
		14th carried out a similar task on their left. Also shelling a long communication trench leading up from PIETRE Cross-roads.	
	11.10	14th silenced a trench mortar which was active near SUNKEN ROAD	
	During day	Hostile artillery were surprisingly silent, 15 cm. from direction of Ht. POMMEREAU was somewhat active round RUE BACQUEROT.	
	During night	7th and 14th fired salvos at frequent and irregular intervals on communication trenches specially allotted to each battery.	
		14th also fired on places where enemy's wire had been damaged.	
22.9.15	7 a.m. to 5.30 p.m.	7th again bombarded PIETRE Cross-roads and four specially selected houses	
	7.5 p.m.	14th fired at few rounds on German trenches for reference.	

(9 29 6) W 2794 100,000 8/14 H W V Forms/C. 2118/11.

Instructions regarding War Diaries and Intelligence Summaries are contained in F. S. Regs., Part II. and the Staff Manual respectively. Title pages will be prepared in manuscript.

WAR DIARY
or
INTELLIGENCE SUMMARY. [illegible]
(Erase heading not required.)

Army Form C. 2118.

Hour, Date, Place	Summary of Events and Information	Remarks and References to Appendices
22.9.15 [illegible]	[illegible] Contd. a deliberate bombardment of [illegible] [illegible] [illegible] EAD [illegible] [illegible] H.E. [illegible] shells [illegible] with good [illegible] [illegible] EAD [illegible]	
2[illegible]	[illegible]	

[illegible] W 2[illegible] [illegible] H W V Forms/C. 2118/11.

Instructions regarding War Diaries and Intelligence Summaries are contained in F. S. Regs., Part II. and the Staff Manual respectively. Title pages will be prepared in manuscript.

WAR DIARY or INTELLIGENCE SUMMARY. IV Bde. R.F.A.

(Erase heading not required.)

Army Form C. 2118.

Hour, Date, Place	Summary of Events and Information	Remarks and References to Appendices
23·9·15 During night	7th & 14th again fired burst of fire at irregular intervals on their allotted stretches of roads & communication trenches. In addition to this 14th Bty fired on places where wire had been cut during day. One section of 14th went into action in a position previously prepared at M 34 a 9·8	
24·9·15 4·40 to 4·50 a.m.	7th & 14th carried out early morning registration.	
5 a.m. to 6 p.m.	14th bombarded houses in M. 36 a & M 36 b & surrounding trenches.	
	14th also carried out registration of advanced section.	
7 a.m to 6 p.m.	7th shelled houses selected, & support trenches in M 36 d.	
During day	Hostile artillery very quiet 15 c.m. near BAS POMMEREAU put 3 shells 100x short of 14th Bty position & 6 into DUCK'S BILL.	
During night	7th & 14th fired as before on selected targets, including places where wire had been cut, also a slow rate of fire on Salient M36 a 4 4	
	66th having finished their allotted task under O.C. IX Bde. R.F.A. again came under command of O.C IV Bde. R.F.A.	
	7th 14th & 66th teams & wagons brought up to orchards in RIEZ BAILLEUL.	

(9 29 6) W 2794 100,000 8/14 H W V Forms/C. 2118/11.

Instructions regarding War Diaries and Intelligence Summaries are contained in F. S. Regs., Part II. and the Staff Manual respectively. Title pages will be prepared in manuscript.

WAR DIARY
or
INTELLIGENCE SUMMARY. IV Bde. R.F.A.
(Erase heading not required.)

Army Form C. 2118.

Hour, Date, Place		Summary of Events and Information	Remarks and References to Appendices
During night 24th/25th		Infantry took up positions in fire trench from COLVIN trench to S. MOATED GRANGE Street from right to left as follows:—	
		2/3rd GURKHAS with Lieut G. KIDDLE attached as advanced F.O.O.	each with telephone party
		2nd LEICESTERS with 2/Lt. C.D. PARCELL	
		2/8th GURKHAS with 2/Lt. A.A.D. KEMPSTER	
		Capt. J.C. CROCKER was attached to GARHWAL Bde as Bde. Liaison Officer	
25.9.15	5.40 p.m.	Mine under ~~sal~~ MAUQUISSART Salient at M 30 a 2.5 exploded.	
	5.50	Cluster of rockets sent up which marked beginning of operations.	
	5.50 to 5.59	Shelled enemy's front line trench 7th from M 26 c 85.75 to M 26 a 5.1, 14th M 26 a 5.1 to M 26 a 4.5, 66th M 26 a 4.5 to M 20 c 5.0 also one section shelled concrete house at M 20 c 5.0. Each Battery sweeping 1° right & left to ensure overlapping, maintained rate of Section fire 10 secs.	
	5.59	Infantry getting out of trenches.	
	5.59 to 6.1	7th, 14th & 66th all lifted 100x and maintained same rate of fire	
	6.1 to 6.3	7th lifted another 100x.	
	6.1 to 6.4	14th & 66th both lifted another 100x.	

(9 29 6) W 2791 100,000 8/14 H W V Forms/C. 2118/11.

Instructions regarding War Diaries and Intelligence Summaries are contained in F. S. Regs., Part II. and the Staff Manual respectively. Title pages will be prepared in manuscript.

Army Form C. 2118.

WAR DIARY
or
INTELLIGENCE SUMMARY. IV Bde. R.F.A.

(*Erase heading not required.*)

Hour, Date, Place		Summary of Events and Information	Remarks and References to Appendices
25·9·15.	6·3 to 6·10 p.m.	7th switched two sections to front line M 36 c 1·5 to M 36 c 3·8 and one section on communication trench M 36 d 4·8½ to M 36 d 7·7.	
	6·4 to 6·10	14th lifted to enemy's reserve trenches M 36 d 4·9 to M 36 d 1½·4	
		66th " " " " M 36 d 1½·4 to S 6 a 8·9	
	6·10	F.O.O. reported that smoke made observation very difficult and that hostile artillery was very quiet.	
	6·10 to 6·20	7th, 14th & 66th all continued barrages at rate of section-fire 30 secs.	
	6·20 to 6·35	7th, 14th & 66th " " " " " " 1 min.	
	6·35 to 6·40	7th, 14th & 66th " " " " " " 2 mins.	
	6·45	7th, 14th & 66th " " " " " " 3 mins.	
	7·00	Hostile artillery became more active especially their 15 c.m. Howitzer. 2/Lieut. C. B. PARCELL, who was with O.C. 2nd LEICESTERS in our fire trench, was wounded and evacuated to hospital later in the day.	
	7·20	66th formed barrage M 30 d 8·6 to M 30 d 10·0 at rate of section-fire 2 mins.	
	7·50	Enemy established a strong barrage on HOME COUNTIES trenches and heavy howitzers shelled trenches near MOATED GRANGE.	

Instructions regarding War Diaries and Intelligence Summaries are contained in F. S. Regs., Part II. and the Staff Manual respectively. Title pages will be prepared in manuscript.

WAR DIARY
or
INTELLIGENCE SUMMARY. IV B[illegible] R.F.A.
(Erase heading not required.)

Army Form C. 2118.

Hour, Date, Place		Summary of Events and Information	Remarks and References to Appendices
	9.00 p.m.	2/Lieut A.A.D. KEMPSTER killed whilst crossing from our line to [illegible] [illegible] O.C. [illegible] [illegible]	
25.9.15	9.[illegible] a.m.	[illegible] position at [illegible]	
	[illegible]	[illegible]	
	9.20	[illegible]	
	[illegible]	[illegible]	
	[illegible]	[illegible] moving up [illegible] along [illegible]	
	[illegible]	[illegible]	
	[illegible]	[illegible]	
	12.20 p.m.	[illegible]	
	5.00	[illegible]	

[illegible] W [illegible] 100,000 [illegible] H W V Forms/C. 2118/11.

Instructions regarding War Diaries and Intelligence Summaries are contained in F. S. Regs., Part II. and the Staff Manual respectively. Title pages will be prepared in manuscript.

WAR DIARY or INTELLIGENCE SUMMARY. IV Bde. R.F.A.

(Erase heading not required.)

Army Form C. 2118.

Hour, Date, Place		Summary of Events and Information	Remarks and References to Appendices
25·9·15	5·00 p.m.	to salient M 30 c 0·4 with, 14th Bty in liason, 39th GARHWAL RIFLES.	
	6·00	Orders:— Bde. Liason Officer to remain at GARHWAL Bde. Headquarters, advanced F.O.O. withdrawn but Battery Liason Officers to stay at Infantry Battalion Headquarters at night as usual.	
	7 to 11	Batteries did not fire.	
	9·30	Two sections of 7th withdrawn to former position	
	11 p.m. to 2·30 a.m.	7th fired intermittant bursts on communication trenches M36 d 33 to M36 d 6·5.	
		14th " " " " M36 d 6·5 to M36 b 7·9	
		and tram-way junctions in N 31 a and N 25 c.	
		Ammunition expended by IV Bde. R.F.A. during last five days Shrapnel 5500 and H.E. 1400.	
26·9·15	11·00 a.m.	14th fired a few rounds on two suspected O.Ps.: house at N 32 a 6·1 and sand-bags in tree at N.W. corner of the wood in T 1 b.	
	2·00 p.m.	7th 14th & 66th wagon-lines withdrawn to PONT RIQUEUL.	
	3·00	2/Lieut A.A.D. KEMPSTER buried at PONT DU HEM. Rev. R. IRWIN read the service and Maj. Gen. JACOBS (G.O.C. MEERUT DIV)	

(9 29 6) W 2794 100,000 8/14 H W V Forms/C. 2118/11.

Instructions regarding War Diaries and Intelligence Summaries are contained in F. S. Regs., Part II. and the Staff Manual respectively. Title pages will be prepared in manuscript.

WAR DIARY
or
INTELLIGENCE SUMMARY.
(Erase heading not required.)

Army Form C. 2118.

Hour, Date, Place	Summary of Events and Information	Remarks and References to Appendices

Army Form C. 2118.

Instructions regarding War Diaries and Intelligence Summaries are contained in F. S. Regs., Part II. and the Staff Manual respectively. Title pages will be prepared in manuscript.

WAR DIARY
or
INTELLIGENCE SUMMARY. IV Bde. R.F.A.

(Erase heading not required.)

Hour, Date, Place		Summary of Events and Information	Remarks and References to Appendices
28.9.15.	8.30 p.m.	60th Bde. relieved DEHRA DUN Bde. on front line by extending its right to SUNKEN ROAD. 6th Shropshires in liason with 14th.	
		JOLLUNDUR Bde. took over line by extending its left to SUNKEN ROAD. 2/2nd Gurkhas remained in liason with 7th.	
	During night	Section 7th relieved by section 81st and withdrawn to wagon lines.	
	" "	" 14th " " " 2nd " " " " "	
		2/Lieut. F.L. CASSIDY, Corps of Interpreters (on return from hospital) to 4th Black Watch.	
29.9.15.	10 a.m.	Composite 7th & 81st under command of O.C. 7th Bty. handed over to control of O.C. XI Bde. R.F.A.	
		Composite 14th & 2nd under command of O.C. 14th Bty. handed over to control of O.C. XIII Bde. R.F.A.	
	During night	Two sections of 7th to wagon lines, O.C. 7th handing over to O.C. 81st on relief by two sections of 81st.	
		Two sections of 14th to wagon lines, on relief by two sections	

Instructions regarding War Diaries and Intelligence Summaries are contained in F. S. Regs., Part II. and the Staff Manual respectively. Title pages will be prepared in manuscript.

WAR DIARY
or
INTELLIGENCE SUMMARY. [illegible]
(Erase heading not required.)

Army Form C. 2118.

Hour, Date, Place	Summary of Events and Information	Remarks and References to Appendices
[illegible].9.15 During night	[illegible] 2[illegible] [illegible] [illegible] in command until noon 30.9.15. [illegible]	
30.9.15 2 p.m.	[illegible]	
" "	[illegible] IX [illegible]	

[illegible]

[illegible] Bde [illegible]

Serial No. 38.

Confidential

121/7601

War Diary

of

IV Brigade R.F.A.

FROM 1st October 1915 TO 31st October 1915

Instructions regarding War Diaries and Intelligence Summaries are contained in F. S. Regs., Part II, and the Staff Manual respectively. Title pages will be prepared in manuscript.

WAR DIARY
or
INTELLIGENCE SUMMARY. IV [illegible]
(Erase heading not required.)

Army Form C. 2118.

Hour, Date, Place	Summary of Events and Information	Remarks and References to Appendices
[illegible]	[illegible]	
	[illegible] MILLER [illegible]	
	[illegible] W. CUNNINGHAM [illegible]	
	[illegible]	
[illegible]	[illegible] CAPEL [illegible]	
	[illegible]	

[illegible]

Instructions regarding War Diaries and Intelligence Summaries are contained in F. S. Regs., Part II. and the Staff Manual respectively. Title pages will be prepared in manuscript.

WAR DIARY
or
INTELLIGENCE SUMMARY. IV Bde. R.F.A.
(Erase heading not required.)

Army Form C. 2118.

Hour, Date, Place		Summary of Events and Information	Remarks and References to Appendices
4·10·15	During day	66th enlarged gun-emplacements to enable guns to fire over an extended front. Continued registration also fired 6 rounds at an enemy working party.	
5·10·15	" "	66th completed alterations to gun-pits & continued registration.	
	" "	14th carried out registration & retaliated on bomb-gun.	
6·10·15	12·30 p.m.	7th marched from CAPEL BOOM to wagon lines at MESPLAUX	
6·10·15 7·10·15	During day	14th & 66th continued registration, weather bad & everything very quiet along the front.	
7·10·15		7th came under orders of O.C. 17th Bde. R.G.A. to act as counter-battery covering from VIOLAINES to LA BASSEE Canal.	
		2/Lieut G. GORDON from 14th Bty. to IV Bde. A.C.	
		2/Lieut W. CUNNINGHAM from IV Bde. A.C. to 14th Bty.	
8·10·15	6 p.m.	Two sections of 7th came into action in GORRE MARSH at F 11 b 3·6; thick fog registration impossible.	
		14th Bty retaliated for hostile bombing.	
		66th Bty did not fire.	

(9 29 6) W 2794 100,000 8/14 H W V Forms/C. 2118/11.

Army Form C. 2118.

Instructions regarding War Diaries and Intelligence Summaries are contained in F. S. Regs., Part II, and the Staff Manual respectively. Title pages will be prepared in manuscript.

WAR DIARY
or
INTELLIGENCE SUMMARY.
(Erase heading not required.)

Hour, Date, Place	Summary of Events and Information	Remarks and References to Appendices
[illegible]	[illegible]	
[illegible]	[illegible]	
	[illegible] WILLOT.	
[illegible]	[illegible]	
[illegible]	[illegible]	
[illegible] 4.00 p.m.	L.X. of 7th ([illegible]) moved [illegible] position [illegible] with [illegible] from A22 d 42 [illegible]	
	[illegible]	
[illegible]	L.X. of [illegible] BRICK [illegible]	
	18th [illegible]	
	36th [illegible] LA BASSEE [illegible]	
	[illegible] CANAL [illegible]	
	[illegible] 6th B.ty.	

W 5794 [illegible] H.W.V. Forms C. 2118/11.

Instructions regarding War Diaries and Intelligence Summaries are contained in F. S. Regs., Part II. and the Staff Manual respectively. Title pages will be prepared in manuscript.

Army Form C. 2118.

WAR DIARY or INTELLIGENCE SUMMARY. IV Bde. R.F.A.

(Erase heading not required.)

Hour, Date, Place	Summary of Events and Information	Remarks and References to Appendices
12.10.15 During night	Batteries were supplied with ammunition for bombardment of 13th.	
13.10.15 Noon	Heavy artillery opened fire on Fosse No. 8., 7th & 66th. assisted with enfilade fire from noon to 8.00 p.m.	
1.00 to 2.00 p.m.	Smoke barrage along front of Indian Corps.	
2.00 p.m.	11th Corps attacked Fosse No. 8 and 4th Corps H13 a 4.2	(near Hulloch)
3.00 "	14th Bty retaliated on fire trench for hostile bombing.	
~~7.00 "~~	~~7th Bty shelled positions of three suspect~~	
7.00 to 8.30 p.m.	7th Bty. shelled three positions of suspected hostile batteries.	
During night	66th Bty kept up steady rate of fire on allotted targets.	
14.10.15 During day	7th Bty checked registration, 14th located & shelled an enemy bomb-gun and 66th fired at irregular intervals of LA BASSEE bridge to hamper enemy's communications. 66th Bty experienced great difficulty with two of the guns handed over to them. Buffer springs found to be warped & compressed below condemning limit. The exchange of guns with other Batteries is not considered at all advisable.	

(9 29 6) W 2794 100,000 8/14 H W V Forms/C. 2118/11.

Army Form C. 2118.

Instructions regarding War Diaries and Intelligence Summaries are contained in F. S. Regs., Part II, and the Staff Manual respectively. Title pages will be prepared in manuscript.

WAR DIARY
or
INTELLIGENCE SUMMARY.
(Erase heading not required.)

Hour, Date, Place	Summary of Events and Information	Remarks and References to Appendices

W 2794 - 10,000 - 8/14 - H W V - Forms/C.2118/11.

Instructions regarding War Diaries and Intelligence Summaries are contained in F. S. Regs., Part II, and the Staff Manual respectively. Title pages will be prepared in manuscript.

WAR DIARY
or
INTELLIGENCE SUMMARY. IV Bde. R.F.A.
(Erase heading not required.)

Army Form C. 2118.

Hour, Date, Place	Summary of Events and Information	Remarks and References to Appendices
19.10.15	7th Bty ceased to act as counter-battery and was attached to IND 1 Artillery Group under O.C. 9th Bde. R.F.A.	
6.30 p.m.	Centre Section of 7th Bty withdrawn from SIDBURY HILL to wagon line.	
20.10.15	66th continued barrage as yesterday, otherwise quiet day.	
21.10.15	66th continued barrage as before.	
20.10.15	2/Lieut E.D. DOYLE joined from C.1. Res. Bde. posted to 66th Bty.	
21.10.15	Quiet day for 7th & 14th Bty. Batteries & Column moved to new wagon lines 7th at R 33 d 9.2, 14th at X 3 c 4.8, 66th at X 3 a 2.8 and Column to R 26 c 5.4.	Bethune combined sheet.
	Centre Section of 7th Bty came into action at S 7 b 2.7 alongside C/88 Bty (4 guns) [same position occupied by 7th for NEUVE CHAPELLE] Right & Centre Section of 14th Bty to wagon line on relief by C/87 Bty.	
22.10.15	C.X. of 7th Bty registered FERME DU BOIS & laid out normal lines. Other sections of 7th did not fire.	

Army Form C. 2118.

Instructions regarding War Diaries and Intelligence Summaries are contained in F. S. Regs., Part II. and the Staff Manual respectively. Title pages will be prepared in manuscript.

WAR DIARY
or
INTELLIGENCE SUMMARY.
(Erase heading not required.)

Hour, Date, Place	Summary of Events and Information	Remarks and References to Appendices

Instructions regarding War Diaries and Intelligence Summaries are contained in F. S. Regs., Part II. and the Staff Manual respectively. Title pages will be prepared in manuscript.

WAR DIARY
or
INTELLIGENCE SUMMARY. IV Bde. R.F.A.
(Erase heading not required.)

Army Form C. 2118.

Hour, Date, Place	Summary of Events and Information	Remarks and References to Appendices
24.10.15 4.00 p.m.	Group [IV Bde Batteries & 61st How. Bty] from O.C. 88th Bde.	
6.00	Left section of 66th on relief by 12th Bty relieved remaining section of A/88 Bty.	
7.30	Right section of 7th Bty came into action at S 7 b 2.7.	
During Day	14th and 61st carried out registration.	
	IND III Artillery Group in liason with Garhwal Bde.	
	7th Bty on right in liason with 2/3 Gurkhas holding from PIPE TRENCH to FARM CORNER	
	14th on left with 39th Garhwals from FARM CORNER to CINDER TRACK.	
	66th as "swinger" in touch with both 7th & 14th, & able to cover the whole front of IND III section. 61st covering whole front	
25.10.15 During day	7th, 14th & 61st carried out registration.	
1.30 p.m.	14th retaliated on enemy's fire trench with 12 rounds for 3 from hostile 15 c.m from direction of LORGIES which fell on our support trenches	
10.50 p.m.	12 77 mm shells were fired along the RUE DU BOIS.	
26.10.15 During day	The light was exceptionally good and 7th, 14th 66th & 61st	

Instructions regarding War Diaries and Intelligence Summaries are contained in F. S. Regs., Part II. and the Staff Manual respectively. Title pages will be prepared in manuscript.

WAR DIARY
or
INTELLIGENCE SUMMARY. [illegible] Bde. R.F.A.

(Erase heading not required.)

Army Form C. 2118.

Hour, Date, Place	Summary of Events and Information	Remarks and References to Appendices
[illegible]	[illegible]	

9 2966 W 2791 190,000 5/14 H W V Forms/C. 2118/11

Army Form C. 2118.

Instructions regarding War Diaries and Intelligence Summaries are contained in F. S. Regs., Part II. and the Staff Manual respectively. Title pages will be prepared in manuscript.

WAR DIARY
or
INTELLIGENCE SUMMARY. IV Bde. R.F.A.
(Erase heading not required.)

Hour, Date, Place		Summary of Events and Information	Remarks and References to Appendices
28·10·15		2/Lieut. A.W. FOSBROOKE-HOBBS (Tempy Com) joined from 3. A. Res. Bde. R.F.A. and was posted to 7th Bty.	
29·10·15	11·30 a.m.	14th shelled a M.G. emplacement in fire trench at S 16 a 6·½	Trench Map 36 S.W. 3.
	1·00 p.m.	14th registered COUR D'AVOUE, MOULIN D'EAU & fire trench S 22 c 2·7 to 5·3.	
	1·20 -	Hostile 15 c.m shelled LEICESTER LOUNGE and EMBANKMENT trench to which 14th retaliated on enemys fire trench.	
During afternoon		7th 66th & 61st continued registration of various points.	
6·00 p.m to 4·30 a.m.		Five times, each for a period of half an hour, during the night a 77 mm fired on LA COUTURE at about two minute intervals)	
29·10·15		Lieut. G. KIDDLE struck off strength of 7th Bty on W.O. letter.	
30·10·15	11·30 a.m to noon	14th registered several undamaged houses near S 23 d 0·1	
	12·15 p.m.	77 mm & 15 c.m shelled EMBANKMENT trench and support line of IND III "B" but ceased when 14th & 66th retaliated	
	2·35 p.m.	15 c.m. shelled communication trenches of IND III "A" but stopped firing when 7th Bty retaliated with two battery salvos on their front line trenches between S 16 a 6·6 & S 22 a 3·4.	

(9 29 6) W 2794 100,000 8/14 H W V Forms/C. 2118/11.

Instructions regarding War Diaries and Intelligence Summaries are contained in F. S. Regs., Part II. and the Staff Manual respectively. Title pages will be prepared in manuscript.

WAR DIARY
or
INTELLIGENCE SUMMARY.
(Erase heading not required.)

Army Form C. 2118.

Hour, Date, Place	Summary of Events and Information	Remarks and References to Appendices
[illegible]	[illegible]	

[illegible] W 2794 [illegible] H W V Forms/C. 2118/11.

R.F.A
1915

C O N F I D E T I A L

WAR DIARY

OF

The Officer Commanding, IV Brigade R.F.A.

FROM November 1st 1915 TO November 30th 1915

(VOLUME ---)

Instructions regarding War Diaries and Intelligence Summaries are contained in F. S. Regs., Part II. and the Staff Manual respectively. Title pages will be prepared in manuscript.

WAR DIARY

or

INTELLIGENCE SUMMARY.

(Erase heading not required.)

Army Form C. 2118.

Hour, Date, Place	Summary of Events and Information	Remarks and References to Appendices

Army Form C. 2118.

Instructions regarding War Diaries and Intelligence Summaries are contained in F. S. Regs., Part II. and the Staff Manual respectively. Title pages will be prepared in manuscript.

WAR DIARY or INTELLIGENCE SUMMARY. IV Bde. R.F.A.

(Erase heading not required.)

Hour, Date, Place		Summary of Events and Information	Remarks and References to Appendices
4·11·15	1·5 p.m.	Several 15 c.m. shells fell in RUE DU BOIS about 200x N.E. of the SAVOY, 14th retaliated on enemy's front line trench.	
	1·40	A large number of 77 m.m. shells were fired, apparently from about S 23 c 8.8, in IND II Section, 14th shelled enemy's fire trench in retaliation, 66th also retaliated on S 16 d 2.8.	Trench map 36 S.W. 3.
	2·20	14th shelled FME DU BOIS where snipers were active.	
	3·10	66th dispersed enemy working in trenches behind FME DU BOIS	
	During day	7th fired on FMES COUR D'AVOUE and TOULOTTE.	
	7·00	1/9 Gurkhas relieved 1st Seaforths on IND III "B" in liason with 14th.	
		Lieut. T. R. ANDERSON joined from "J" Bty. and was posted to 7th Bty. taking over the duties of acting Captain.	
5·11·15	10·10 a.m.	66th fired 8 rounds on a working party near FME. DU BOIS.	
	1·10 p.m.	66th fired 12 rounds on suspected enemy O.P. at S28 b 2.5	Trench map 36 S.W. 3.
	2·15	7th checked their night-lines.	
		Lieut. A. H. MAC ILWAINE joined from "K" Bty. R.H.A. and was posted to 14th Bty. taking over duties of acting Captain.	

(9 29 6) W 2794 100,000 8/14 H W V Forms/C. 2118/11.

Army Form C. 2118.

Instructions regarding War Diaries and Intelligence Summaries are contained in F. S. Regs., Part II. and the Staff Manual respectively. Title pages will be prepared in manuscript.

WAR DIARY

or

INTELLIGENCE SUMMARY.

(Erase heading not required.)

Hour, Date, Place	Summary of Events and Information	Remarks and References to Appendices

Instructions regarding War Diaries and Intelligence Summaries are contained in F. S. Regs., Part II. and the Staff Manual respectively. Title pages will be prepared in manuscript.

WAR DIARY or INTELLIGENCE SUMMARY. IV Bde. R.F.A.

(*Erase heading not required.*)

Army Form C. 2118.

Hour, Date, Place		Summary of Events and Information	Remarks and References to Appendices
8·11·15	10·00 a.m.	66th Bty shelled probable O.P. in house at S 22 a 6·6.	Trench Map 36 S.W. 3.
	3·00 to 4·00 p.m.	Hostile artillery active — 77 mm from direction of the RUE DU MARAIS shelled fire trench of IND III Section while another 77 mm not located shelled the support trenches, also a 10·5 c.m. and 77 mm fired on RUE DE CHAVATTES & KING GEORGE'S ROAD. 7th & 14th retaliated on enemy's fire trench. 66th shelled house, at S 28 b 6·5 used as an O.P., where enemy were seen to enter before and leave hurriedly during firing.	
	9·00 p.m.	4th Seaforths relieved 1/9 Gurkhas in IND III "B" in liason with 14th.	
	During night	Section of C/89 Bty relieved Section of 61st Bty.	
9·11·15		Very quiet day all round.	
		Major W.P. PAYNTER from 14th Bty left to command "Q" Bty R.H.A.	
		Capt. D.G.C. RUTHERFOORD assumed command of 14th Bty. R.F.A.	

(9 29 6) W 2794 100,000 8/14 H W V Forms/C. 2118/11.

Instructions regarding War Diaries and Intelligence Summaries are contained in F. S. Regs., Part II. and the Staff Manual respectively. Title pages will be prepared in manuscript.

Army Form C. 2118.

WAR DIARY
or
INTELLIGENCE SUMMARY.

(Erase heading not required.)

Hour, Date, Place	Summary of Events and Information	Remarks and References to Appendices

W 2W6 W 2794 100,000 5/14 H W V Forms/C2118/11.

Army Form C. 2118.

Instructions regarding War Diaries and Intelligence Summaries are contained in F. S. Regs., Part II. and the Staff Manual respectively. Title pages will be prepared in manuscript.

WAR DIARY or INTELLIGENCE SUMMARY. IV Bde. R.F.A.

(Erase heading not required.)

Hour, Date, Place	Summary of Events and Information	Remarks and References to Appendices
25·11·15 10·30 a.m.	In the grounds of the Chateau at LILETTE, H.R.H. The Prince of Wales, after inspecting representatives of units, delivered the message from H.M. King George V to the Indian Corps. IV Bde sent ten representatives (Lt. Col. S.F. STALLARD was C.R.A. Lahore Division) O.C. [Major J.W. PARRINGTON] and Adj. [Lieut. C.C. MIMS] O.C. 7th Bty [Lieut. G. KIDDLE] and one man. O.C. 14th Bty [Capt. D.G.C. RUTHERFOORD] and one man. O.C. 66th Bty [Major M.R.H. CROFTON] and one man. O.C. IV Bde. A.C. [Capt. W.G.C. COCKADAY] and one man.	Sheet 36A 1/40,000 N 22 b 9·1
28·11·15	Lieut. A.H. MacILWAINE from 14th Bty. to R.A. Hd. Qrs. as Staff Capt. R.A. Lahore Division. Lieut C.C. HADDEN took over duties of Acting Capt. 14th Bty.	
29·11·15	IV Bde. marched from THEROUANNE to billets in villages of NEDONCHELLE and FONTAINE LEZ HERMANS about 6 miles S.W. of LILLERS.	

Army Form C. 2118.

WAR DIARY
or
INTELLIGENCE SUMMARY. IV Bde. R.F.A.
(Erase heading not required.)

Instructions regarding War Diaries and Intelligence Summaries are contained in F. S. Regs., Part II. and the Staff Manual respectively. Title pages will be prepared in manuscript.

Hour, Date, Place	Summary of Events and Information	Remarks and References to Appendices
30·11·15	Lieut G. BARRY. A.V.C. left to join 61st (How) Bty. R.F.A. [illegible] Div Arty.	

C. C. Mims. Lt. R.F.A.
Adj IV Bde. R.F.A.

War Diary for

December 1915

4th Brigade RFA

Instructions regarding War Diaries and Intelligence Summaries are contained in F. S. Regs., Part II. and the Staff Manual respectively. Title pages will be prepared in manuscript.

WAR DIARY

or

INTELLIGENCE SUMMARY.

(Erase heading not required.)

Army Form C. 2118.

Hour, Date, Place	Summary of Events and Information	Remarks and References to Appendices

www.ingramcontent.com/pod-product-compliance
Lightning Source LLC
Chambersburg PA
CBHW082007220426
43670CB00014B/2574

* 9 7 8 1 4 7 4 5 3 5 1 1 3 *